****

Interview with a Terrorist

By James Rosone
With Miranda Watson

****

Published in conjunction with Front Line Publishing, Inc.

Copyright Information

ISBN: 978-1-957634-25-8
Sun City Center, Florida, USA
Library of Congress Control Number: 2022904110

Dedication

I would like to dedicate this book to all the men and women who served in Iraq, and in particular to those who served as interrogators. Regardless of whether the decision to go to war in Iraq was the right decision or not, we all went there in service of our country putting our lives on the line. The media may have mischaracterized our job overseas, but I stood beside you and know that you played a central role in this conflict, and that you served with distinction.

To my wife—you helped bring me through one of the toughest experiences of my life, and the inner conflict that began after I arrived home. I know that my deployment was not easy on you. It could not have been fun to have our phone calls interrupted by mortar attacks…yet, you persevered. Thank you for staying the course.

Finally, thank you to all of those who prayed for me while I was overseas, and after I came back home. Without your support, things would be very different now.

Table of Contents

New Notes for the Second Edition

Several years have passed since we published the first edition of this book under the title of *Dinner with a Terrorist* in 2010. Since then, a lot has changed in the world, and many things within myself have developed. In these past six years, I have completed my MBA and a Master of Science degree at the University of Oxford; I have also spent two additional years working in Iraq as a contractor and four years in identity intelligence across Europe, Eurasia and the Middle East, hunting and tracking Islamic extremists. I have gained a lot of knowledge and perspective since I originally released the first book and have spent a lot of time reflecting on what I have learned since then. These experiences led me to write a second edition to my story to make it more relevant to the world today.

Throughout this book, you will notice portions of information that have been blacked out. This is data that I have shielded from the public because it was potentially sensitive to national security. Unlike certain politicians with fancy lawyers, I do not have the ability to share information that might even be considered borderline classified without facing prosecution.

Introduction

The word *interrogator* conjures up all kinds of images of torture and abuse—the kind of stuff you see Jack Bauer from *24* do to people, like hooking them up to a car battery and shocking them, or sticking bamboo shoots under their fingernails. I guess I did not fully understand the stigma of being an interrogator until after I returned from Iraq and people would ask what I did there. The surprised and disgusted looks people back home would give me when I told them about my job were rather disturbing. I could tell that they suddenly viewed me or this profession as something evil or wrong, yet it is far from that. Maybe they felt that I would somehow expose all the wrongs they had ever done or uncover a dirty secret—in any case, aside from people asking me if I ever tortured or waterboarded anyone, the conversation would usually end fairly quickly, and they would move on to talking with someone else. I think the problem may lie more in that people do not really understand what an interrogator does. Most people don't really have any concept of how important interrogators—and the information that they collect—are in the fight against radical Islam.

I want to provide a glimpse into what it is like to be an interrogator, and to hear, see, and feel what we deal with. We are normal people, thrust into unimaginable situations and forced to make judgment calls that may save or end a life. I want to humanize the US military interrogator to the world and let people know that we are not the savage, degenerate monsters the media makes us out to be. We are average people asked to do a dirty job that most people would rather not know about. We hear and see things that no one should ever have to experience—yet we do it because it is a job that is critical to the security of our country and to our success in combating terrorism and radical Islam.

During the Revolutionary War, the Minutemen did not conform to the previously established rules of battle. Instead of forming up into regimented units, wearing bright military medals, they snuck through the woods in clothing that blended into the trees. This change in tactics utterly confounded the British and was definitely one of the factors that led to our winning independence. Today, we face a similar change in strategies. The war against radical Islam simply cannot be won by the use of conventional force alone. Terrorists hide in plain sight, cloaked in the veil of anonymity. This new secret war will be won or lost in the dark shadows of the night, with a few spectacular moments in between. Information is our strongest weapon. Americans were not prepared for this kind of war, but this battle will ultimately be decided with human intelligence. This is why the role of the interrogator is so crucial in the world today.

Chapter 1
A Call to Arms

I was in the Air Force when a call went out for volunteers to step up and assist the Army in fighting this shadowy war as human intelligence collectors, known to the outside world as interrogators. I knew nothing of human intelligence and had no clue what an interrogator actually did. I'd seen the stories about prisoner abuse by Army military police at Abu Ghraib as they'd unfolded in the media, but somehow, I had the sense to know that this was not indicative of the actions of the vast majority of American interrogators.

Despite my lack of knowledge, when I heard the announcement go out, I felt called to this mission. Perhaps I was idealistic or naïve, but I have always wanted to be a part of something greater than myself; more importantly, I wanted to have the opportunity to really make a difference. My wife and I took some time to pray and see if this was what God wanted me to do. It probably sounds strange, asking God if he wanted me to be an interrogator, but that is what I did. All through the Bible, there are examples of how God took the most insignificant people and used them to accomplish the most amazing things, and I figured, why not me? I didn't think of myself as a strong and powerful Christian, or even that religious, but I knew I wanted to do this mission.

I didn't fully understand what I was getting myself into, and if I had, I'm not sure I would have volunteered. At the time, I felt a peace about signing up for this assignment. However, this peace was just the calm before the storm that God was about to take me through. I was going to begin a dark journey that would take me face-to-face with some of the greatest enemies our country has ever seen, and God would pit me against some of the most malicious and wicked people one could possibly imagine. I would be walking into the valley of the shadow of death, and I would sit down for dinner with evil, the likes of which I could only begin to dream up in my mind. My faith would be tested and pushed to the brink; yet in all of it, my faith would see me through and open up the minds of my detainees like nothing else could.

Despite the challenges to come, I completed the paperwork to volunteer for a special duty assignment as an interrogator in the fall of 2005. Four months later, I received my orders to leave the Air Force and attend training at the US Army Intelligence training center in Arizona, where we would be integrated into a joint military unit for this eighteen-month mission.

As I exited the plane in Tucson, Arizona, the blistering heat of the southwest desert smacked me in the face like a hair dryer on max heat, and the reality of going to Iraq started to set in. As we drove in to Fort Huachuca, one of the oldest active bases in the Army, the landscape was littered with cactus plants and tumbleweeds. It was a different type of desert, but a foreshadowing of the future nonetheless.

Some of the buildings along the ridgeline dated back to World War I, but I would be spending most of my time in barracks that had been built in the 1980s and modular trailer units for instruction. I drifted off into daydreams about what I thought my new life would entail. I was about to be grafted into a world that most never dream of entering—a world of secrets, deception, and mystery. I barely slept the night before we began training, thinking of all of the spy movies and TV shows I had seen over the years. But the first day of interrogation training was surprisingly low-key.

The instructor who walked through the door seemed more like an accountant than James Bond, and we spent most of the day talking about the basics of constructing questioning plans. As we left for the barracks that evening, I could tell some of the guys were a little disappointed. Many of them were adrenaline junkies that were born for the military life. They were much more likely to run through a forest playing paintball in their spare time than read a book—yet we were finding out that our main weapon for the next year and a half would be our words and our minds, not bombs and bullets.

Things picked up for us a bit after we started learning specific tactics that we could use. As we dusted off our two-inch-thick manuals, we would go through each strategy at length, poring over scenarios and possible questions that leveraged each technique.

I was so eager to soak in all the knowledge my teachers had to offer that some of the conversations are permanently etched in my memory. I still remember my instructor laying out how to conduct the "love of family" approach. He told us, "If a detainee has family, then use it—get him to cooperate by probing him with questions like, 'Who is going to take care of your family while you're in prison?'"

You could hear the pens and pencils writing frantically around the room as the interest level picked up. We wrote as quickly as possible as the teacher continued with more examples. "Ask your detainee, 'Don't you care about your family? Who is going to take care of your little daughter and provide food for your baby son if you're in prison?'"

I could tell that questions like this would wreak havoc on a person's emotions, especially if the detainee had a large family and was the sole provider.

Then, as though sensing hesitation in the room, our instructor explained, "You may think this cruel, but I will tell you that it is extremely effective. No one wants to be separated from their family or know that their family is becoming destitute. It makes the detainee feel a sense of hopelessness and desperation. That's when you can get him to trade information in exchange for his freedom or the promise of his freedom."

For a split second, I felt sorry for the men I would be using this technique on. I'm pretty close with my family, and the thought of them becoming homeless because I couldn't provide for them would certainly test my emotional will to resist. But then I remembered that most of these men were terrorists who would eagerly kill me if given the chance. With my mind focused on the task at hand, I finished scribbling notes and got ready for the following topic.

I looked up to see the word "futility" written on the board. It was the name of the next approach. That technique was all about illustrating to the detainee the pointlessness of their resistance, that the only way out was going to be through cooperation. The instructor explained that this technique would be most effective if we could show the detainee the mountain of evidence gathered against him.

The instructor pointed to one of the students. "Jim, you'll be my detainee, and you are a Sunni."

"OK," replied the pupil.

The instructor jumped right into the role of interrogator and asked, "So, Mr. Omar, who's in charge of the government here?"

"The Shi'a."

The teacher smiled, then continued, "So what do you think will happen when you go before a Shi'a judge and the evidence is laid out before him?"

The student got into his role and indignantly replied, "That's not fair!"

"Life's not fair," the instructor calmly replied. "It wasn't fair for the people who died because of your actions."

Breaking character for a moment, the instructor explained, "If this had been a real interrogation, you would have just broken the law by threatening to harm the detainee."

We all looked at each other in confusion and then collectively asked, "What do you mean?"

"According to the new DoD field manual on interrogations, you as an interrogator are not allowed to threaten or coerce a detainee into providing information. By asking the detainee who controlled the government and the courts and what might happen to him if he was handed over, you just connected the dots for the detainee as to what may happen to him rather than letting him connect the dots on his own.

"The context of the words used in an interrogation is just as important as the approach," our instructor said. "Instead of asking him who controls the government and the courts or what may happen to him, inform the prisoner, 'If you are unwilling to cooperate, then you are of no value to me or the US military. You will be handed over to the Ministry of Interior and the Iraqi criminal system.'"

We all tried to catch the subtle differences in the wording. The instructor elaborated, "The prisoner knows exactly what will happen to him if he is handed over. However, you have not crossed the line and connected the dots *for* him. You have allowed him to do that on his own."

We discussed the nuances of what constituted a threat and what was acceptable within the limits of the law for what felt like days. When we were finished, I felt exhausted.

As we got out of class for the day, a bunch of the guys wanted to head over to a bar. I've never been much into that scene, so I bowed out. A couple of the other guys went with me to a nearby steakhouse, and we tried to lighten the mood for a little while. It was pretty heavy to think that the slightest slip of the tongue could result in disciplinary action and even possible court-martialing. It was best not to dwell on it. For a couple of hours, we were no longer interrogator students but just a few guys enjoying some good grub. We drove back to the base as the sunset painted the sky with brilliant hues of orange and pink that stretched over the mountain line. This was one thing about the desert that was truly spectacular.

The next day started the circus all over again. We picked up right where we had left off. The instructor began, "All right, folks. Let's build on yesterday's topic. Once you have enlightened the detainee on the futility of his ways, you can move on to the 'incentive' approach by offering your prisoner a chance to make things right by providing information.

"For example, you could suggest, 'Mr. Omar, if you give me the information I need, then I can put in a good word for you when your case goes to court, or we may be able to use you as a source and you could work for us. Wouldn't you like that?'"

The wheels were quickly turning in my head. It seemed to me that these promises would be far more effective after they had already been brought to the point where they realized that not cooperating would be detrimental to them. A one-two punch would be much more successful than either tactic on its own.

The instructor seemed to be thinking the same thing as he went on, "For some of your prisoners, the idea of help in the criminal justice system just won't go very far with them. However, say this detainee is one of those guys that the 'love of family' approach is working well with—in that case, you could offer him additional letters home to his family, or maybe even phone calls home.

"If you have a single guy with no family who just doesn't care about that, there still may be an incentive that might work for him. Believe it or not, after a while in these camps, the thought of simple comfort might be enough to move the pendulum. The guys get tired of living in these five-hundred-man rooms that the general population is kept in. The idea of a single cell or a cell with just one roommate could be very appealing. Throw in some better food and TV privileges, and you may have a bird that's ready to sing.

"All of these techniques, 'love of family,' 'futility,' and 'incentive,' are far more effective when used in combination with each other, and you have to pay attention to what is working and what is not. Be ready to switch streams if needed."

****

The days blended together. Every day, we were up and standing at formation at 0445 in the morning. PT started by 0500 and lasted ninety minutes. Then there was breakfast, followed by four hours of training. Next was lunch at the mess hall, and another four hours of class. It was a lot of information to cram into our heads. Fortunately, most evenings we didn't have any homework to bring back to the barracks, which gave us a little time to let the day's lessons sink in. I even had time to play a few rounds of Madden football on my Xbox. Other guys would frequent local bars. We all had our ways to decompress.

On the weekends, some of us would travel to Tucson and check out the latest gadgets at Best Buy, or maybe take a trip to Tombstone to see the shoot-out at the OK Corral. I really enjoyed touring Bisbee—the copper mines were interesting, but I felt restored by the lush greenness there.

After a few weeks, the monotony of the classroom was finally broken up. We'd take part of the day training in the field, learning how to read maps or administer first aid. We would practice tourniquet techniques on each other— obviously without fully tightening them—or we would review how to call the nine-line medevac. Other times we would spend the entire day at the rifle range, learning how to effectively zero a rifle, practice shooting from a moving vehicle, or just doing basic target practice. There were pop-up targets at the rifle range that looked like little green soldiers, and they would appear at twenty-five meters, one

11

hundred meters, or all the way out to three hundred meters. The closer targets stayed up less time than the ones that were farther away. If we hit a target, it would go down—otherwise, it would count as a miss. We'd be given forty targets and forty rounds to hit them with, and we'd need to hit twenty-six of them to qualify.

Once we had established a baseline of marksmanship, we ran scenarios in improvised villages where we would breach a room, learning how to move and cover each other. Then it was time for convoy training. We learned how to position our gun turrets to get maximum coverage, and then we moved on to strategies of what to do if attacked. We would have mere seconds to decide whether or not we'd be able to push through the attack and escape, or whether we'd all have to get out of the vehicle and engage. When we did have to get out, we'd need to work effectively as a unit to ensure that we didn't all get picked off one by one.

As we continued in our interrogation coursework, we began to have more time outside of standard classroom learning. We would practice what we had been taught in an improvised interrogation booth located in a shipping container. Our instructors pretended to be detainees who had been captured while participating in terrorist activities. Their personalities completely transformed, and it was easy to believe they were our enemies. They constantly pushed our buttons, attempting to find the points that would incense us the most: our families, our faith, the values we held deeply. Nothing was safe or off-limits. They tried to make it as realistic as possible so that when we got to Iraq and this became real, none of this would faze us. Some of the adrenaline junkies got so sucked into the reality of it all that they exploded in anger during the mock interrogations. Others got so turned around that the detainee was interrogating the interrogator before they knew what had happened. After most of us failed the exercises, we started to learn some self-control and how to deal with a mentally sharp and determined foe.

For the rest of the course, we kept learning techniques and putting them into practice. The more simulations we completed, the more real the whole the situation seemed. As we progressed through training, I visualized myself running these approaches with the detainees that I knew I would soon be interrogating.

The training started to stretch out into the nights and weekends. There were morning road marches and combative training techniques, similar to MMA. A few times, some of the guys got a little carried away while sparring and ended up with a few bruises. Now we were prepared to stack tight in alleyways and move as a unit in all sorts of situations. We put in a ton of hours practicing combat situations as well as our craft. We were all getting a little tired.
****

Around the Fourth of July, something horrible happened. On the holiday weekend, one of my fellow students had been riding his motorcycle in Tucson when a vehicle turned right in front of him. He didn't have time to slow down, and he was thrown headfirst off his bike. Even though he had been wearing a helmet, he didn't survive the accident.

This tragedy shocked our systems. We had all just seen him the day before, and then suddenly he was gone. He had been one of those guys who was open and approachable with everyone, so we all felt that we had lost a friend. Even when others weren't, he had always been friendly to me. He was a helpful, mature guy, and it was truly a loss. The reality of our mission hung over us like a cloud. Our own mortality was at stake. We weren't guaranteed to survive the year in Iraq, or not to come home maimed if we did.

The Army was surprisingly understanding about it all. Normally, it just would have been announced, but they allowed us to have a short memorial service. There was a eulogy, and then we all walked by a rifle and bayonet that had been propped in the dirt next to a helmet to pay our respects. In the dayroom of our barracks, the guys all made a shrine to honor our fallen comrade, with pictures of all of us together. We talked about how he would have made a great interrogator because of the ease with which he related to people.

Several months had gone by already, and while in general I had been interested by the training, I was also missing my wife. We had just gotten married in March of 2005, making us still newlyweds. We had already been through a lot with the passing of her mother two months after we were married, and this deployment was going to be another challenge for us to endure.

Although we had been given many valuable tools for our deployment, the training was far from over. The next phase of our preparation involved the learning of spy craft, which is the art of spotting a source and recruiting them to spy or gather information for you. We learned how to go beyond basic interrogations to identify and enlist individuals to work for us, as well as assess their potential value from an intelligence standpoint. We were now learning information that was the type of stuff you see in CIA movies.

We learned how to establish a dead drop to pass information. The best places were spots that were easy to see but hidden in plain sight—for example, under a rock. Or a source could put a note inside of a bag and drop it into a trash can. As long as you knew when this would happen, you could readily pick it up without detection. If a face-to-face was needed, a source could leave a chalk mark on a designated building, signaling a meeting at a preset place and time.

It was honestly sort of fun to practice some of these techniques. We would practice meeting at a coffeehouse, sitting back to back at different tables, talking quietly so the rest of the patrons couldn't hear what we were saying. Other times, we would don disguises such as sunglasses, hats, ratty clothes or black-tie fashion, and play a chess game in the park. It was difficult to play the game and also speak casually at the same time, to avoid suspicion.

I felt like a light went on in my head during this course. I remember the moment it happened—we were sitting in the classroom when our instructor explained that it was not enough to simply interrogate someone.

He said, "You also have to ascertain if they actually possess any information of intelligence value. Whether a detainee cooperates or not—it's your job to overcome any barriers to collaboration. However, if the subject doesn't have any information that is of intelligence value, then move on to the next detainee until you find someone with intelligence value. Your goal is not to determine the detainee's *guilt*—your goal is to find information that the combat forces can use to capture or kill his colleagues in terrorism."

Our training quickly moved to a field exercise as we repositioned away from the base and deep into the Huachuca Mountains. For this particular part of the training, we moved beyond the interrogation booth to makeshift villages—complete with markets, mosques, and residential areas—and enacted dozens of real-life scenarios. We ran an eighteen-hour operational tempo to simulate what it would be like when we got to Iraq. Our instructors, who were now villagers and terrorists alike, gave us specific assignments to collect intelligence out amongst the villagers, and at random times throughout the day, a "prisoner" would be brought to the tent we were operating out of.

We also completed foot patrols with military police and infantry soldiers. Our instructors issued us 210 rounds of blank ammunition, so we could "shoot" back at anyone who attacked us out on patrol. Our opposition force was also armed with blank ammunition, including artillery simulators. When the instructors would pull the pin, a loud whistling, shrieking noise like the sound of an artillery projectile flying overhead would begin, and then a loud BOOM would go off, reverberating through the ground. This would help train us to respond to both direct and indirect fire.

One day, while en route to a village, my group suddenly found itself under attack by AK-47s and rockets. I began to shoot back, and then a group carrying M4s barraged us from several other positions. The deafening sound of a wall of guns being discharged overpowered all other senses.

Now I had to try to fight my way out of what had become a well-planned ambush. As my patrol returned fire, an instructor would walk up to one of us and say, "You are now wounded," forcing us to perform medical treatment on a comrade while still under enemy attack. The assault lasted between two and five minutes, which was just long enough for me to mentally run through what I should do if this had been a real attack.

At the end of the scenario, we had to drag a fellow soldier who had been deemed "dead" back to our camp. The reality of what could happen sank in as we had to leave him outside the village for more than an hour as part of the rules of the simulation while we continued on with our initial mission.

I quickly found that patrols were never going to be boring. On another day while on patrol, I was shopping at the market, striking up a conversation with one of the locals and trying to gain their trust. Out of nowhere, an individual who was selling vegetables at a little stand on the side of the road opened fire on me and my group.

In the blink of an eye, one of the members in our patrol was killed and another was wounded. Before I had a chance to kill the attacker, he surrendered, and I was forced to take him prisoner. Now we had to conduct an on-the-spot interrogation of the detainee to try to determine what terrorist organization he worked for. The fact that we were still in the village and in an area that was extremely hostile didn't make it any easier either, so I stood guard and provided security while one of my teammates questioned the detainee.

Out of the corner of my eye, I could see the interrogator growing extremely frustrated that he wasn't getting any information from the attacker. After a while of this building rage, the platoon leader in charge of our group came up to the prisoner and tried to get him to talk as well. When that didn't go so well, he yelled at the prisoner to get the man talking. I'll never forget watching the prisoner as he was sitting there on his knees with his hands behind his head—and suddenly he spat on the interrogator. At that exact moment, my teammate totally lost control and "executed" the detainee with his rifle.

That fiasco immediately ended our exercise. Everyone got their heads chewed off by our instructors. I can almost still hear them screaming at us about how executing a prisoner was not only a violation of the law of war but was also a criminal offense, for which we would go to prison.

I think that exercise reached its goal of putting as much pressure on an interrogator as possible to see if they could handle the burden and do the right thing—unfortunately, in this case, the answer was no. In a way, I'm glad it played out like it did because it proved to be an invaluable training experience for us. We all started to recognize our own breaking points, and most of us figured out what we should do when we saw ourselves reaching them.

After each day's patrols, we sat around in our tent writing up our reports about the day's events and what we had learned. We would discuss with our instructors what had gone right and what had gone wrong, devising strategies of how we could do things better and what we would do next time. This daily process of conducting patrols and writing reports was repeated for two long weeks, testing us on everything we had learned in class and during the exercises.
****

The man who would become my roommate in Iraq, "Red," had an interesting case during training. The scenario was simple enough. A male detainee refused to talk until his wife, who had also been arrested, was brought to him. Such a demand might seem innocent to a layperson, but Red knew that the prisoner could use that time together to instill fear in her that she was not out of his reach, frightening her into silence. Red did not allow the detainee to see his wife, but he used the prisoner's purported anguish to get some information out of him. After about thirty minutes of trying to have a rational discussion with the man, Red made a radical decision.

He realized that he knew enough about the detainee and his wife that he could figure out who she was by process of elimination, even though he didn't know her name. There were only fourteen women anyway—it had to be one of them. He took a picture of the man and then sent him back to lockup. Then he headed on over to the women's block.

Red pulled one of the women aside and took her to the cage. He showed her the photograph and then bluntly explained, "This man is scheduled for trial and execution of the sentence tomorrow morning."

Those words had been chosen very carefully. Using the word "execution" in conjunction with the man's picture gave a false impression through a language barrier, without actually communicating a threat. Since the conversation was clearly recorded, Red was legal.

He went on to explain, "The only way that this man can avoid trial tomorrow is if his wife will come forward and give us information."

The woman took the picture back with her into the prison, which was easy to accomplish since the guard had been in on the tactic and allowed her to have the photo. Ten minutes later, a sobbing, hysterical woman came rushing to the front of the group. She screamed, "Please, don't kill my husband!"

Because of the misunderstanding in the language, the woman was sure that her husband would be executed, even though that threat had *never* been made. Within moments, Red had collected all the information that he needed—mission success. Through this case, we all learned that what people don't know or understand is just as important as what they do.
****

The work was exhausting, and Arizona's 110-degree heat in August was relentless. Even the breeze wasn't refreshing—it felt like I was walking around with a hairdryer on my face. Between the eighteen-hour workdays, the overpowering weather, and the eight-mile road march with a ninety-pound pack just to get there, the exercise really put a strain on us physically and mentally. Each person's limits were thoroughly tested. Fortunately, like all the previous training I had gone through, this too was about to end.

Following our four and a half months of basic HUMINT training, I was sent home for an all-too-brief ten-day break. It was nice to spend some much-needed time with my family and decompress. Since I was stationed in Tampa, Florida, my wife and I took a trip to Universal Studios and spent some time alone, having fun touring the park, watching movies in the theater and having some great dinners. Those ten days went by faster than a flash of lightning, and before I knew it, I was back on the plane heading back to Arizona for our second phase of training.

The Air Force made a great decision and sent our group to the Enhanced Analyst and Interrogation Training Course, which was the pinnacle of all interrogation schools one could go through. This second phase of training was a much lighter schedule, 0800 to 1500 hours, similar to being in college. Of course, our evenings were occupied, between convoy training, close-quarter combat training, foot patrols, and everything else one goes through when preparing to deploy.

Our instructors for this course had all been to Iraq and had fresh experience as interrogators. They were a storehouse of information that I fully planned on exploiting. One of our instructors had just completed a two-year contract working as an interrogator in Guantanamo Bay, Cuba, and another instructor had just retired from the Army as a CW3, or chief warrant officer, level three, with the Special Forces. Both instructors had an immense amount of practice interrogating some of the toughest terrorists who had ever been caught.

As we sat in class one day, soaking in the wealth of wisdom, one of the instructors asked us a question I will never forget. "What if your prisoner starts to talk?"

At first, his question caught me off guard because I assumed that would be a good thing, but his tone implied that there was cause for concern.

He warned us, "If that happens, you need to be ready—ready to ask all of the follow-up questions, and more importantly, to recognize when the detainee is about to break, and then close in for the kill."

He went on to explain, "Sometimes a prisoner will be on the verge of talking, and then the interrogator does something *stupid* that causes him to regain his composure and shut up. I've seen a guy get exasperated just as the flood was about to start, storm out of the room and say, 'Well, I guess you're just going to spend some more time in the camp then.' Or, even worse, the prisoner starts talking and the interrogator goes after the guy too hard, yelling and screaming at him.

"I've also seen prisoners talk, and the interrogator just wasn't prepared with all of the necessary follow-up questions. Most interrogators encounter immense amounts of resistance and expect to get little if anything of value. They don't fully prepare in-depth questioning guides in case the detainee does break."

I thought to myself, *I won't let myself fall into that trap.*

Slowly and steadily, I was learning how to become a professional manipulator. I was figuring out how to steer a discussion to gain the information I was looking for, weaving between effective closed- and open-ended questions. I was starting to feel like I could have someone talking about a secret before they even knew it. As we continued practicing what we had learned through the role-playing scenarios, I could feel myself developing my own style and techniques.

Besides the obvious, these simulations also taught me how to stay within the laws and regulations, dodging through the complicated legal spiderweb to achieve the desired outcome. The 2005 Detainee Treatment Act had created a number of wording problems for interrogators, as mentioned earlier. We had to be extremely careful not to threaten a detainee physically or verbally, or threaten the detainee's family in any way. A threat, or even a perceived threat, could end an interrogator's military career and even result in criminal charge. I was amazed at how complex and legalistic the interrogation process had become. It reminded me of how the Johnson Administration micromanaged the Vietnam War, all the way down to approving specific targets that could be bombed.

In the wake of the Abu Ghraib prison scandal, which incidentally was the fault of the guards and not the interrogators, Senator John McCain had championed the 2005 Detainee Treatment Act to make sure that no one would have to endure what he had experienced as a prisoner in Vietnam. While I do not condone that sort of violence or humiliation, the law went far beyond restricting actual torture into the realm of political correctness, ultimately tying the hands of the intelligence community. I want to qualify this accusation by saying there are plenty of means to obtain information from a detainee without torturing him. In fact, torturing a detainee is perhaps the worst thing an interrogator can do. It puts a question mark on the intelligence gained because you cannot be sure if the information was legit or if the prisoner said what you wanted to hear to make you stop hurting him. That's the main reason I feel torturing a prisoner is not effective. However, after these attempts to make the interrogation process not just humane but politically sensitive, several methods of handling detainees that I do *not* believe constitute torture are now deemed restricted approaches.

I do not discount John McCain's service to our country. He volunteered to go to Vietnam at a time when the war was unpopular, and as a result he was captured and spent many years as a prisoner in unsavory conditions. However, as a politician, Senator McCain was ineffective at advancing the situation for frontline military personnel. He did nothing concrete to improve veterans' healthcare at the VA, and his meddling into the minutiae of the Iraq War tied our hands to the point of having us fight with one hand tied behind our backs while we jumped on one leg.

It used to be that a prisoner could be put into separation with relative ease. This technique prevented a detainee from talking to his counterparts and developing a cover story in the detainment camp, or from being indoctrinated with interrogation resistance techniques. Slowly, as a detainee would be interviewed, the holes in his cover story would become apparent, and as he slipped up, the true information would come to light. All an interrogator had to do was request permission from the officer in charge of the facility to have the newly arrived detainee placed into a solitary confinement cell.

However, after McCain and his fellow legislators had gotten involved in the daily workings of our jobs, we were forced to have a *two-star general* sign off on any request to have a prisoner put in separation for a thirty-day period. If we wanted to put the detainee into separation for another thirty days, bringing the total number of days in separation up to sixty days, we were going to need a *four-star general* to sign off on the request. And should we determine that the prisoner needed to be in separation longer than sixty days, nothing short of *presidential* approval would allow that to happen.

Another technique we were told was restricted is called the "Mutt and Jeff." This is basically the "good cop, bad cop" that you see the police using on a daily basis, in which two separate interrogators play opposing roles. One person plays the nice, gentle good guy who is there to help the prisoner, while the other person is the mean ogre who wants to hand the prisoner over to the Iraqi police rather than keep him in US custody. Rather than being left to the discretion of the interrogator assigned to the case, this approach could only be authorized by a colonel. I found it preposterous that this interrogation technique is OK for US police to use on a regular basis against American citizens, yet it is a restricted approach for the military when interrogating a terrorist. It's strange how an Al Qaeda terrorist has more protection in a war zone than an American citizen has when being questioned by the police or federal agents in our own country.

There is another, more unique approach called the "false flag," in which the interrogator impersonates someone from another country. Instead of stating that you are a member of the American intelligence community, you simply inform the detainee that you are a part of the Canadian intelligence service, or whichever country's intelligence service you feel you can adequately pull off. It's an effective technique because a prisoner may feel more at ease talking to a Canadian intelligence officer than an American intelligence officer—but once again, it may only be used with the approval of a colonel. This micromanagement of our interrogation approaches was far-reaching, and I felt that it was going to seriously hamper our efforts to collect intelligence.

The thought of possibly going to jail because I made a threat, or simply a perceived threat, to a detainee who had just killed several Americans made me nervous and angry. These people are monsters and mass murderers, and yet they were being given more protections during an interrogation than I would have if I were arrested by the police or FBI. Our law enforcement routinely uses the perception of threats and numerous other coercive techniques to obtain confessions from people they interrogate—but if I did that as a military interrogator to a terrorist, I could lose my career in the military and face criminal charges of my own.

After learning of all the consequences of breaking regulations, I was determined not only to stay within the boundaries of what I felt was morally right, but to keep my nose as clean as possible in regard to the rules. I was going to have to focus on the most effective methods that fit into the box that had been given to me. Fortunately, there was plenty of ammunition left; I just had to get creative.

One day while we were sitting in the classroom, one of my instructors gave us some insight into one of our potential tools. He said, "Preparing the detainee's mental and emotional state prior to and during an interrogation is often one of the most important aspects to the interview. It helps to set his mind and emotions up and weaken his psyche or resistance level."

I thought about an introductory psychology course I had taken in college, and I almost laughed as I remembered the story of Pavlov conditioning those dogs to salivate at the sound of a bell. That got my mind to wondering what we could use in a detainee's environment to condition them.

We reviewed the various incentives that would be available to us as interrogators and ran some scenarios to explore which ones would be the most useful, depending on what the prisoner was responding to. I wondered what negative consequences I could use when I had a tough nut to crack, given the extreme limitations we were under legally.

This was when I learned about the SHU or separation housing unit. Its use is unfortunately restricted, so we would need to obtain permission in advance to use this technique. However, it is extremely effective because it isolates the prisoner from the rest of the population, thereby reducing the effectiveness of the detainee's cover story and his ability to resist during interrogations. The SHU itself is a unique room. It has no windows, is painted completely yellow, and is lit by a soft yellow light. There is a small metal bed with a sleeping mat, one pillow, and a blanket. Though this room may not sound like much, it has an incredible psychological effect on a person. The color yellow has been shown to make a person mentally uneasy; to further amplify this effect, the soft yellow light is left on twenty-four hours a day. Couple this with complete isolation from anyone but the interrogator, and it is an exceptional psychological tool to use, *if* you could get it approved.

The detainee would be given one hour a day in an open recreational area, where he could kick a soccer ball or just walk around in the open air of an enclosed six-foot-by-twelve-foot area, still in isolation. When the prisoner was moved from his cell to the rec yard, his daily doctor visit, or to his interrogation, he would be asked to kneel, facing away from the door with his hands on his head. Then the guard would come in and zip-tie his hands and place earmuffs over his ears and an eye shade over his eyes. Next, the guard would place a black hood on the prisoner and guide him to his scheduled destination. This would place the detainee in a continual state of disorientation and confusion, which would further add to the isolation he would already be feeling. During the detainee's entire time in the SHU, the only people the prisoner would see were the doctor and the interrogator.

The instructor did caution us, "It is imperative to have a well-thought-out plan for how you are going to use the detainee's isolation to break him down during the interrogations if you're going to place him in the SHU. You've already learned about the time limitations of this technique, so you need to use it wisely and effectively."

After that class was over, we all went to dinner to chew on what we had just learned. It was coming close to the end of our training, and I knew that I needed to take away every piece of wisdom I possibly could.

One morning after breakfast, I sat down across from one of our instructors and said, "So, you've been in the field. Besides all the stuff that you've been teaching us in class, what do you wish someone had told you before you went overseas?"

He smiled a little bit, pulled his chair closer to the table, and leaned in as if he were telling a secret. He began to paint a picture. "Imagine you're knocking at the door of someone's home. This is the first stage of the interrogation, when you first approach the case and begin to develop your plan of action for how you're going to get past knocking on the door. Once the door has opened, you're talking to the man who owns the house. This is the second stage of the interrogation, an open dialogue between the detainee and you as the interrogator. The next step is the most difficult step to achieve—getting the detainee to allow you into his home—or in this case, his head, where the information lies.

"This is the step where most interrogators stop. They have gained entry into the detainee's head and have discovered some basic yet valuable information from this first room the detainee has shown you when he invited you in. But this isn't the last step—far from it."

I leaned in as he continued, "The fourth and final stage in the interrogation is to get the detainee to take you on a *tour* of his home—or in this case, his head. You want to get the detainee to fully disclose everything and allow you to walk around freely in his mind. This is when you gain the most valuable intelligence."

He leaned back and sighed. "Putting this metaphor into practice in the fluidic environment of a combat zone and under immense pressure was rather difficult, and at times extremely frustrating. But that's how you'll become a truly great interrogator."

I took in everything I could and mulled it over that evening as I looked out at the Arizona sunset. There were a lot of guys in my group who seemed to be satisfied with the status quo, but that wasn't me. This wasn't just a job or an adventure I had signed up for; I really wanted to make a difference, as naïve as that may sound.

Before we left the advanced course, our instructors taught us how to work with our analyst counterparts. I would be forming what has been dubbed a "tiger team." By pairing an analyst with an interrogator, the chances of identifying and then capitalizing on information increases dramatically.

An analyst is an individual who is trained in all-source intelligence, which means they are a jack-of-all-trades when it comes to intelligence. They are typically a generalist in their field, but they have great analytical and research backgrounds. Their role would be to help us paint the big picture and allow us to see the forest for the trees. Their researching abilities could come in handy later if I ran into complex cases in Iraq, which was sure to happen. Though an analyst cannot directly participate in an interrogation, they can provide the interrogator with additional questions to ask or pass a note on a specific point that needs to be clarified. This second set of eyes and ears could be the difference between a successful interrogation and an unsuccessful one. Before we left Arizona, I wasn't sure what to make of my counterpart, but in time, I would come to both love and loathe my analyst.

I now found myself transformed from a regular joe into a fully trained professional interrogator, and it was time to take everything I had learned and use it for real. This wasn't going to be a practice run. The exercise wouldn't stop if I did something wrong. Now I'd be putting all the techniques I'd learned to the test. I prayed that the results would be positive.

Chapter 2
Heading to the Sandbox

After spending four days at home and acquiring the last pieces of equipment and weapons from our home units, we boarded planes across the US all heading toward Norfolk, Virginia, from where we would ultimately deploy to Iraq. My wife and I said our goodbyes at the airport and kissed for what could be the last time. As I walked down the gangway to the aircraft, I honestly felt afraid and I wanted to cry. I steeled my resolve and pushed my emotions back into their box. I had to set my focus on the mission at hand and hope for the best.

As we arrived at the great naval base that is Norfolk, I was awed by the sheer size of one of the supercarriers that was in port. There were also several other ships that had just arrived, and we could see all the family members waiting at the end of the pier for their loved ones to walk off the ship. A couple of interrogators and I actually walked up into one of the larger troop carriers and had a look, until a Navy guy saw us and started asking questions. He kindly guided us off the ship.

Our flight left the following evening, and we made our first stopover in Bangor, Maine, to refuel. There was a very patriotic group of people from the local VFW there with American flags to greet us and wish us luck. It felt good to have some people wishing us well, especially since, in all reality, none of us knew for sure if we were going to come home.

We made two more layovers, one in Shannon, Ireland, where everyone in the Air Force had some final Irish beers. Being Air Force, we had different rules about drinking, and until we arrived in Kuwait, unlike our Army brethren, we were allowed to drink. Our next layover was in Leipzig, Germany, before we finally made it to Kuwait City. Although it was evening when we arrived in Kuwait, the one thing we felt immediately was the heat. It had to be well over ninety degrees, and it was a safe assumption that it was going to be a lot hotter during the day.

Our bus ride to Camp Buehring, which is located in the middle of nowhere, was rather comical. The trip should have taken about an hour—Kuwait is not that big of a country. Instead, our journey took close to three hours as our guide got lost and we meandered hopelessly through the desert. After making several sharp turns in the dark, we started to wonder if we were ever going to arrive at our destination. However, we did eventually reach the camp.

Camp Buehring is the last stop most forces make before entering Iraq. We went to the range and zeroed our rifles and conducted some additional convoy training. Finally, we completed exercises on improvised explosive devices and the current tools being used to defeat them. We were shown PowerPoint briefing after PowerPoint briefing filled with pictures of IEDs that had been found in guardrails, under asphalt on the road like a pothole patch, inside of dead animals on the side of the road, in piles of trash, etc. Terrorists and insurgents can be pretty smart creatures, although they have used their intellect for evil purposes, in order to create deadly devices that are *very* difficult to identify. I started to wonder if I was going to survive my deployment without being maimed; wires can be hard to spot at high speeds. Fortunately, there are some new tools in the American tool chest to counteract IEDs. I won't elaborate too much here, but it definitely gives us an advantage. After a few terrifying days at the camp, being inundated with the many ways we could be killed or maimed, we were ready to deploy into Baghdad.

There isn't anything routine about a deployment to Iraq. I found this out firsthand on my first of many flights there. As we got closer to Baghdad International Airport or BIAP, our C-17 cargo aircraft suddenly lurched into a combat descent. Out of nowhere, the plane dropped a thousand feet at once. It felt like my stomach had lifted up into my throat. Then we made several tight turns, one right after the other. For a moment, the plane slowed down, and I felt a bit of relief…until I realized that we were climbing again. Seconds later, the plane was free falling at high velocity again. My backpack floated for a few seconds before landing back in my lap. My suffering finally ended when the aircraft slammed into the runway.

Anyone who, unlike me, loves crazy roller coasters at theme parks would have adored this grueling ride. One of my neighbors seated next to me explained that the planes land like this in order to make them harder targets to shoot at. It only made me want to bail out as soon as humanly possible.

Though I felt like I wasn't going to make it through that first plane ride, I had officially begun my tour in Iraq. As I stepped off the plane and looked around for the first time, I had no idea what to expect. I was scared, nervous, and a long way from home. I was also anxious to see the place we would call home for the next year.

Once we had collected our belongings, we boarded a minibus that drove us over to Camp Stryker. As we plodded along, the landscape whirred by in a monochromatic scene of desert colors and military camo—everything seemed to blend together. The large, sprawling camp seemed to be full with the 3,500 soldiers that were living there at the time. Little did I know that before I left, there would be over 10,000 staying there, or one full combat brigade and remnants of two others. Soon enough, we arrived at the sea of metal boxes where I would be resting my head at night.

I was going to be staying in one of the many PODS, or portable on-demand storage units, which were essentially twelve-foot-by-twelve-foot tin rooms. Although it seems like a small space to be sharing with more than one person for a year, I was grateful that it at least had heat and air conditioning. I spent the remainder of the day getting settled in, unloading my uniforms and getting my individual body armor fitted with my ammo pouches the way I wanted. Once the whole system was set up, it weighed seventy-seven pounds. Let me tell you, lugging that thing everywhere I went provided one exceptional workout. Thus far, things didn't seem so bad, but I was definitely not a fan of the bathroom situation. If I woke up in the middle of the night, I could either walk two hundred yards to a trailer set up as a bathroom with a bunch of stalls, or I could walk fifty yards to a group of port-a-johns.

In addition, I found out that the bathroom trailer had a major engineering flaw. They were designed with a two-inch pipe as the drain, making them prone to continually being clogged. It looked like the portable toilets were going to be the only working solution, and if you've ever used a port-a-potty in 130-degree heat, you'll understand my reluctance to use them. Some guys would use a bottle for those late-night situations, but if you were caught, you would get in trouble, so guys took care to hide such bottles and empty them often.

After I got somewhat unpacked, one of the guys came by and showed me where the chow hall was. It felt nice to get some food in my stomach, and I was surprised at the quality of the grub available. After that, I learned where the buses were that would take me to the adjacent Camp Cropper, which was where I was going to be working. All in all, the first day wasn't so bad...except for the two 240mm rockets that exploded just outside the perimeter of the base. It was my first experience hearing the incoming fire alarms, which wailed up and down like a loud howling banshee. That noise was followed very shortly by the concussion of two loud explosions, and the night briefly turned into day as the rockets impacted just shy of the base, hitting the outer perimeter wall. That wall was only about 1,500 feet from our living quarters. Fortunately, it absorbed all the shrapnel from the explosion.

The second day was a whole new ball game. Being on the night shift, I showed up to work at 2100 hours, ready to be there until 0900 hours the following morning. As I entered the camp, the first thing I noticed was the smell. The stench of 5,000 stinky, sweaty, dirty detainees sweltering in one-hundred-plus-degree temperatures was almost overpowering. The body odor mixed with smells of urine, feces, and garbage was almost too much to handle. The stench of all of those unwashed bodies was enough to make a person want to vomit. Yet this was to become my home, my work, and my life for the next year.

Despite the assault that was happening on my nose, the more I learned, the more I realized that Camp Cropper was an interesting place with many secrets. It was the same facility that was housing Saddam Hussein while he awaited execution, and it also housed several other members of his government and some of the most notorious terrorists we had caught to date in Iraq. The camp sprawled across more than a mile in distance and was home to some 800 US personnel, mostly military police—which constituted the guard force—and about 5,000 detainees.

The camp was broken down into compounds one through five. Compound Five, of course, was the special compound; this is where Saddam was being held, along with the senior leadership of the former Iraqi government. It was also where the senior Al Qaeda members were held. Unlike the other compounds, the prisoners in Compound Five were allowed creature comforts: civilian clothes, regular monitored phone calls, the same food as the guards, and even TV and movies to watch. This was meant to make the prisoners more comfortable and willing to talk. If they chose not to talk, then this comfortable Club Med type of incarceration could quickly be turned into what the other prisoners dealt with: 500 people sharing one compound and one massive building to sleep in.

The camp was also the theater internment facility or TIF, which meant all prisoners captured in Iraq had to go through Baghdad. When a person had been detained, they could only stay at the field level for two weeks before they had to be either released or sent to the TIF. Once they arrived at the TIF, things moved along like an assembly line. The prisoner would be processed into the biometric automated toolset and then screened for intelligence value. Once a determination had been made as to the detainee's level of intelligence value and cooperation, they would either stay at the TIF for interrogation or be sent to Camp Bucca, in the desert of southern Iraq, for long-term detainment.

After being shown around the camp and the building where I would be working, I was introduced to the interrogator I was going to be replacing. I spent a little bit of time talking with him. He was an all right guy, but I could see how beaten down and exhausted he was. He just looked tired. He went through the cases I'd be taking over from him, things to look for, the priority information reports or PIRs, and my area of operation. I was assigned to Multinational Division North as my area of responsibility, and more particularly, the Diyala province, which was in the process of self-destructing just as I was arriving.

My assigned province, like much of the west, north, and northeastern parts of Iraq, was dominated by the Sunnis, though there were two major Shi'a strongholds in Al Khalis and Al Muqdadiya. As many know, the Sunnis were in constant conflict with the Shi'a, who controlled the lower portions of Iraq and most of the border area with Iran. The main points of major conflict where these two religious sects have battled are in Baghdad and the surrounding cities, mostly based on the desire for control of the capital.

My task was simple—obtain as much intelligence about the different terrorist and insurgent organizations in the Diyala province as possible, and assist the combat forces in either capturing or killing them. The task may have been straight-forward, but it was going to be anything but easy to accomplish. The interesting part was separating the insurgent activity from that of the terrorists. The insurgent groups were primarily focused on attacking US forces in order to reestablish the "old order" of things, while the terrorists were just bent on causing as much chaos and killing as they could in order to create as much destabilization as possible. Terrorists hoped to incite reciprocal attacks between the Sunni and Shi'a factions, essentially trying to split the country into an unwinnable civil war. The insurgents limited their attacks to military targets; they were local groups with no international affiliations or ties, and were focused primarily on removing the Americans, who they viewed as occupiers. Groups of interest to me in this category included the 1920th Revolutionary Brigades, the New Ba'ath Party, and the Jaysh al Mahdi, or JAM.

The terrorists, on the other hand, were resolved to cause fear and provoke the overthrow of the government. They tended to have international affiliations and could be transregional in nature. They conducted indiscriminate attacks on military and civilian targets. Some of the terrorist groups present in Iraq included Al Qaeda in Iraq or AQI, Ansar al Sunnah, Ansar al Islam, the Islamic State in Iraq, the Badr Corps and the Iranian Quds Force. They all had two things in common: they all had a propensity for senseless violence, and they were backed by foreign organizations and money.

My head was swimming with all this new information, which was a little bit of a data overload. As I started my third day in Iraq, the transition from a day schedule to that of a nocturnal creature was proving to be challenging. Most of the incoming rocket alarms took place during the day, when I was supposed to be sleeping. Not to mention it was a whole lot hotter.

I pushed myself through the brain fog to do my best to focus on my first real day on the job. It was the first time I witnessed a real interrogation. The booths we used for interrogations were large shipping container boxes divided into three rooms, humble surroundings that were to become my new "office" for the next several months. The booth was simple, only about five feet wide and ten feet long, decorated only by a table, three chairs, and a couple of lights. We sat down in the chairs, and I watched as the interrogator that I would replace asked a suspected Al Qaeda leader a gambit of questions. Although he hit on a host of topics, the entire meeting was of no avail. The detainee just sat there, cried a lot, and repeated, "I don't know anything." After about thirty minutes of fruitless conversation, my tired mentor terminated the interrogation, and we left the booth.

When we were outside, he asked me if I had any questions, and I guess I didn't really know where to begin. I did manage to ask, "Why was the interrogation so short?"

He replied, "There was no need to go any longer—the detainee was not going to provide any information." I couldn't help but feel that this was not the best guy for me to be shadowing for the next couple of days before I jumped in and started interrogating on my own.

Suddenly, without a moment to think, we both found ourselves sprawled out in a nearby bomb shelter. Without warning, we heard a loud scream overhead followed quickly by a blinding flash of light. Our ears were smacked with the sound of several rockets exploding in and around the prison camp. The base was hit with a volley of 122mm rockets, courtesy of Iranian-backed terrorist groups. The intense noise shook the camp like an earthquake, and I found myself feeling closer to my maker.

As it turned out, the rockets themselves hit nothing of importance this time, though they certainly startled us and the detainees in the camp, who had no bomb shelters to run to. Little did I know, this was an ordinary day for those of us serving in Iraq.

I didn't know what to make of the guy I was replacing. I wasn't sure if he didn't care anymore or if he was just tired, but I had been hoping my replacement could provide a lot more help and guidance. The next several days passed by like a blur, and before long, I found myself conducting my first interrogation.

As I walked into the interrogation booth, I was greeted first with the stench of the detainee. As I observed him visually, he looked more like a hobo than a terrorist. He hadn't shaved in close to a month and smelled of urine and feces, even though showers were made available once a day for the detainees to use.

Without hesitation, I walked across the room, shook his hand, and said, "*Salaam al salakem*."

"*Salakem al Salaam*," he replied as he took his seat at the table across from me. My interpreter sat at the head of the table between me and the detainee to facilitate our communications.

As the detainee sat down in his chair across from me, I told him, "I am going to be taking over your case. You will be dealing with me from now on." I could see in his eyes that he wasn't happy to have to start over with a new interrogator, but slowly he resigned himself to the fact that he would have to go through me in the future.

To try and establish some rapport with the detainee, I probed him with some simple questions, trying to work in some questions that I needed him to answer also:

"Why are you here?

Have the guards been treating you well?

What do you know about the terrorists operating in your area?

Have you heard of anyone working with the terrorists?"

The detainee continued to insist that he was just a farmer who had been wrongly accused of being a terrorist.

I had glanced through the detainee's folder prior to the interrogation, and the evidence against him was very incriminating. He had been caught during a raid on his farm that had uncovered a huge weapons cache, containing tens of thousands of rounds of AK-47 ammunition, along with close to one hundred pounds of Semtex and a couple of unused IEDs. My detainee was clearly involved. However, it was unlikely that I was going to gain any information from him. He had already been in the camp for four months and had learned from the other prisoners how not to cooperate with the interrogators. It was apparent that he didn't want to betray the cause he had been a part of. I ended the interrogation after forty-five minutes, realizing that this was going nowhere.

Despite this discouraging experience, I was still full of energy and optimism. During my first week on my own, I was determined to get one of my detainees to cooperate and spill the beans. One of the cases handed over to me was a man who was suspected of being a leader of an Al Qaeda cell in his city. I began with the trifecta: love of family, futility and incentive approaches. For two days, I believed I was actually getting through to the detainee. He was providing some information of value, but he continued to insist he had been set up by people who had a disagreement with him and members of his tribe.

He gave me an elaborate story about why he had been detained and what had happened to him back in his village. His story was actually so convincing that he managed to trick me into believing that he was the victim of terrorists and he had been used as a scapegoat by them. I had failed to evaluate the information that led to his capture, giving me only one side of the truth: his side. Had I spent more time looking at the reports written against him, I would have seen that he was wanted because he had killed several local Iraqi police, and numerous people had reported him as being a cell leader for Al Qaeda.

It was my own fault that I was tricked. I hadn't learned yet what people would do when faced with detainment—the lies they would construct, and the time they had to perfect those lies and cover stories in the camp. This may have been the first time I was fooled, but it surely wouldn't be the last.

Two weeks in, a Special Forces Task Force asked for volunteers from our group to serve with them. Almost everyone in my group put their hands up. We all wanted to believe that we could be a part of some great mission, and despite some early frustrations, we were still excited about our jobs. After interviewing us all, they only selected three from the group—at the time, I was disappointed not to be joining them. However, they kept all the volunteers' names for future reference, so I held out hope that I might be able to join them later.

****

The next several weeks proved to be a rather frustrating time. I was struggling with the stresses of living in a combat zone and dealing with the physical, mental and emotional demands of interrogations. Our base was receiving rocket and mortar attacks on an almost daily basis—some small explosions, some large. It was so random where they landed and what they hit. The sirens would sound, and then we would all run to the nearest bomb shelter, waiting until we would hear the explosions and then the all clear. Then it was supposed to be safe to return to whatever we had been doing.

Unfortunately for me, most of these alarms went off during the day, when I was supposed to be sleeping. Needless to say, this was a rather rude way to be woken out of a deep slumber. We were working almost fifteen hours a day with no days off, and this constantly interrupted sleep was making me irritable and exhausted—and I was only a month into my deployment.

I shared this frustration with one of the physician assistants assigned to my group, and she suggested that I use Ambien to help me improve my sleep. I was desperate, so I jumped at the opportunity to do anything to help my situation. However, I probably should have paid a little more attention to the instructions. A few nights into taking Ambien, I took one of the pills and then sat outside chatting with a few of the guys as I waited for it to take effect. I started to fall asleep but didn't realize that I was dozing off. The guys urged me to go back to my room. Apparently, I picked up my chair and walked directly into a T-wall, smacking my face. Everyone laughed, and I felt nothing. Somehow, I made it back to my POD. In the morning, I didn't remember anything that had happened, but I woke up with a bruised face.

****

A couple of days prior to Thanksgiving, we received some rain. The showers were very welcome because they lowered the temperature and brought the dust level down a lot. However, the precipitation also made everything a muddy mess. The dining facility, or DFAC, had several inches of water and mud in front of the entrance, making it a challenge to get in without soaking your boots in the slippery muck.

For Thanksgiving dinner, our cooks, who hailed from Bangladesh, tried hard to make a traditional Thanksgiving dinner with all the trimmings. Unfortunately, the meal itself was nothing to write home about. Actually, it was rather terrible. Our well-meaning cooks put some kind of cut-up green peppers in our stuffing, which made it taste awful, and they didn't let it cook long enough, so it was extremely soggy. The turkey they gave us was dried out, and even the gravy wasn't very tasty. All in all, it was a rather uneventful Thanksgiving dinner, and one I would rather have gone without.

Slowly, I adjusted to my surroundings, and more importantly, I began to figure out how to interrogate. I also spent a lot of my off time thinking of home and how I was going to get through this next year. As my mind began to wander, I started to read my Bible a lot more. I made a habit of praying before the beginning of each interrogation and at the end of each day for success the next day. God had brought me to this place for a reason, and I wanted to ensure that I was open to hearing His voice and knowing what to do next. I understand that many people are agnostic or don't believe in God, but for me, my religion was one of the few things that helped me feel some semblance of peace amidst the chaos of war.

One day after working the night shift, a friend and I were walking back to our PODS after stopping for some breakfast. It was a beautiful sunrise and the air was still a bit cool as we walked back "home" for some much-needed sleep. Just as we arrived in our living area, we heard a loud whistling noise and a sharp crack against a hard surface. A rocket flew into our POD area and smashed into one of the cement barriers about one hundred feet in front of us. It hit the barrier at just the right angle to break off part of the tip, and it slid down the wall into the dirt, the rocket motor still sizzling. We just stood there frozen for a minute, wondering, *What was that?*

Then it dawned on us that a rocket had just landed right in front of us and hadn't gone off. What we didn't see was that a piece of the rocket had broken off and flown into the room of our night shift supervisor, narrowly missing him and scaring him half to death. We were suddenly jolted back to reality as he came running out of his POD, yelling, "Everyone, run for cover!"

I immediately began knocking on everyone's door, telling them that they had to leave. Though the rocket hadn't gone off, that didn't mean it wouldn't go off later. It wasn't until three hours later when the explosive ordnance disposal team showed up that we learned the detonator had broken off, and that was why it hadn't exploded. All in all, it was a rather rude awakening, as nearly half of our night shift could have been killed or injured had the rocket blown up.

Soon after that, the base commander had a couple of additional counter rocket, artillery, and mortar systems installed in the coverage gaps that they thought they had covered. More often than not, the screaming of, "INCOMING, INCOMING," just created additional panic of an impending blast, rather than the surprise of it just happening without our knowledge. Sometimes it's better not to know when a rocket is heading in your direction than to receive numerous false alarms.

Around that time, Camp Stryker had just installed a Wi-Fi internet service that we could purchase for a convenient price of $59 a month. Of course, it was a sluggish 28 Mbps speed and was turned off anytime a soldier from our camp was killed, which unfortunately happened monthly and sometimes weekly. Despite the high price, I did take advantage of the opportunity. Suddenly, I was able to talk with my wife via Microsoft Live, which turned our computers into video phones. It was absolutely awesome. I could log on and see my wife on the webcam, and we could have an actual conversation, even if there was sometimes a lag. It was the highlight of my week to look at her smile and think of the world outside of the desert dust bowl.

Sometimes our conversations would bring my world to her instead. I remember one day talking on the video phone with my wife when we received one of those rocket warnings. Suddenly, she was hearing the blaring of, "INCOMING, INCOMING!"

Then there was a loud thump—*boom!* A couple of rockets hit the camp. The shockwaves from the blast caused my laptop to bounce off the nightstand where it had been peacefully perched just a moment ago. My wife was quick to ask what had just happened, and like any good husband would do, I told her, "We just got hit with a few rockets. That was the warning alarms and those explosions were the rockets hitting something nearby." Needless to say, she didn't take too well to that, or my nonchalant attitude about it. However, it became something I got used to and just lived with.

Chapter 3
Understanding the Job, and Fatman

Things were really confusing my first month in Iraq. Although we had studied the legal restrictions that we would face once in Iraq, the complex web of regulations proved to be more restrictive than we could have imagined as students. Everything seemed like such a mess, and no one appeared to truly know what was going on. The level of disorganization and lack of leadership and decision-making was rather incredible. Yet somehow, things managed to get done.

I remember one day sitting in the interrogation control element, or ICE, the office where the interrogators and analysts worked, just staring at my computer. I overheard some of the interrogators get excited about finding information on Jaysh al Mahdi checkpoints, or a new phenomenon known as "flash checkpoints" set up by Shi'a militia groups to abduct and kill unsuspecting Sunnis. These particular checkpoints quickly cropped up and then disappeared just as fast.

Being the somewhat cynical person I am, I had to ask myself, *So what? What good is information about a flash checkpoint if no one can track it down before it's gone?*

I tried to hide my apprehension from my fellow interrogators, but in my gut, I just felt like all their joy was unwarranted and a waste of energy. Unless we could figure out who was in charge of the checkpoints or where they were taking the people they kidnapped, the information wasn't of much intelligence value. With such vague information that changed so quickly, there was nothing for the ground troops to act on.

When I took a step back, I realized that my counterparts and I weren't exactly on the same page. If I was going to make a difference as an interrogator, I would need to find not just any information, but information that was of direct intelligence value and would lead to the capture or kill of terrorists or weapons and further our overall cause in Iraq. I spent a lot of time reading the questions inside the endless human collection requirements, or HCRs, to see what information the intelligence community was looking for.

HCRs have built-in questioning guides in them. They're put together by various analysts that work for the Department of Defense or other government agencies back in the States in order to help identify specific areas of interest that a particular analyst or group is watching or monitoring. So, for instance, if the Treasury Department is interested in how terrorists are funneling money into Iraq to support their organizations, they would develop an HCR that would correspond with that topic. Inside that HCR would be a myriad of questions that I and my fellow interrogators could ask about that subject. If, by chance, I managed to get my detainee to answer three or more questions from inside one of the HCRs, then I could write an intelligence information report, or IIR, with the responses to those questions. Once that report was edited and published, it would be sent directly to that analyst group to review and then published on the national intelligence database for other agencies to see and use as well.

As I continued reading the HCRs, I was surprised to find that there were a lot of innocent-natured questions that I could ask my detainees that they might not find too intrusive, and yet this information could still help the cause. Believe it or not, there are government groups out there that want to know about a city's water supply or the level of economic activity going on in a particular area. All this information is used to help guide larger policymaking decisions and determine where additional economic aid or troops may be needed.

I also began to study the priority intelligence requirements, or PIRs. The difference between an HCR and a PIR is simple yet complex. An HCR tends to come from an agency or group that isn't directly involved in combat but needs information to make overall policy decisions. On the other hand, PIRs are generated by commanders on the ground that need to make decisions about how their specific unit will operate. Those commanders are very focused on precise information about their geographical area and aren't as concerned about the big picture. The PIRs also tend to have topics of conversation or discussion points rather than specific questions. Occasionally, obtaining data for a PIR will also answer questions that an HCR is looking to resolve. In that case, the interrogator would get the bonus of having a published report for both the PIR and the HCR, which looks really good for that interrogator's statistics. Of course, that was a major bonus since that was the way we were constantly being monitored by our superiors.

If this information was found to be useful to the intelligence community that had requested it, that organization might follow up with a source-directed requests, or SDRs. Essentially, this is a glorified term for follow-up questions. If the Department of Defense or outside intelligence agencies wanted me to clarify a specific point or verify additional information, that would generate a new IIR. The one major thing I learned from spending all those hours reading HCRs and PIRs was that there was a very wide range of questions and topics I could cover with a prisoner that seemed nonintrusive but were still of intelligence value.

There were numerous government agencies hungry for information. All I had to do now was find a prisoner who could answer the right questions. I didn't need to try and find a weapons cache or additional Al Qaeda members to make a difference—if I found that information, that was great, but there was so much more information that could be gathered. Aside from collecting additional information that was of intelligence value, this type of questioning would enable me to establish rapport with the detainee as I appeared to be interested in helping his community, which would in time lead to him letting his guard down for me as I asked some tougher questions.

This was when I could start to probe for further information regarding who else might be working with Al Qaeda in his area or if he knew of any areas where weapons were being stored. I rapidly learned that intelligence about economic conditions in a province can be just as valuable as information about where explosives were being stored. There's a saying: "If you want a better answer, then ask a better question." This became my motto as an interrogator, as well as a valuable life lesson to take home. My superiors were obsessed with stats—I saw this as an effective way to meet their expectations and still have an impact on the war effort.

As expected, a lot of the men who walked into my interrogation booth were immediately defensive and were quite prepared to tell me their "story." Having read several books on Arab culture prior to my deployment to Iraq, I had learned that Arabs are by nature a sociable culture. They love to talk—well. gossip, really—and drink lots of chai or Turkish coffee.

Almost without fail, when a detainee sat down in front of me, I could guarantee that his first response to any question would be, "I'm innocent." This would be shortly followed by "*Wa Allah Ma'arf*," or "I swear to God I don't know anything." I decided that rather than going right at the detainee about why he had been detained, I would offer to make them a cup of chai or Turkish coffee and offer them a pack of cigarettes. This immediately lowered their guard a bit, and as I began my questioning, they were caught off guard by my intense interest in their village and the well-being of their neighbors.

I would ask questions like, "Does your village have water or electricity shortages? How is the food supply? Are there enough jobs in your village?"

I loved watching the surprise on their faces when I would ask for this type of information as we would sip our chai and I would pour them a refill. As they responded, I would lean in and demonstrate to them that I was listening intently to their response, showing them genuine empathy and concern. Then I probed with some additional questions such as, "Why do you think things are like this?" or "What can the government of Iraq and the Americans do to help fix some of these problems?" At this point, my detainee was usually fairly chatty and relaxed.

That's when I would light a cigarette for him or offer some fresh dates, which I knew that most Iraqis loved.

I would never come right out and ask them about their involvement in terrorism or attacks against US forces. Instead, I would leave them a way out, where they could blame someone else. I'd ask them something like, "Who do you think may be causing the power outages or the water problems in his neighborhood?" This gave them a chance to talk about the terrorists without admitting whether they had worked with them or not. At the end of the day, whether the detainee worked with the terrorists was irrelevant to me. I wanted to know who he knew that was still out there working with the terrorists so we could either capture or kill them. This detainee may have been removed from the population, making him no longer a security threat, but the people he had associated with who were still out there were the ones I wanted to target.

As I said earlier, Arabs are generally a talkative people by nature. They love to gossip and have long conversations, so it became my job to give them an outlet for their chatter. I'd bait them with, "Tell me the latest gossip you heard in the market about who is causing the problems. Who have you heard is working with the terrorist groups?" By asking these types of roundabout questions, I was getting the exact information I was looking for, but from a willing and chatty source. Having these informal conversations over some tea or coffee proved to be an extremely effective way to collect valuable information.

Another way to find out information indirectly was asking how the detainee felt about different terrorist organizations. I'd simply ask, "Are you for Al Qaeda or against them?" Then I'd follow up with, "Why?"

If he had turned on them, it would provide me an opportunity to find out why his allegiance had switched, and I might continue by asking, "Are you willing to do something about these terrorists?" If the answer was, "Yes," I might have identified my new informant.

If my prisoner said he was for the terrorists, I would probe to find out why by asking, "What caused you to lean in that direction?"

Sometimes they would respond with "Money." Other times he would say, "A family member was killed by Coalition Forces." In other cases, he would admit, "I did it because I was threatened." Basically, the reasons that most people worked with Al Qaeda came down to one of two motivations: they had been offered a lot of money to conduct a single attack, or they had a family member who had been kidnapped by Al Qaeda, and they were told if they didn't cooperate, their family member would be killed and the terrorists would then come after the rest of their family.

In many cases, Al Qaeda would offer someone one hundred US dollars to place an IED on the side of the road or to launch an RPG at a vehicle in one of the US convoys. Later in my deployment, I learned that a lot of former Iraqi Republican Guard and Special Forces units were being paid three or four times what they used to get paid by the old regime to use their skills to attack the Americans. This was smart on the part of Al Qaeda as they were recruiting trained and experienced former military and Special Forces soldiers.

What I needed to do was quickly identify with each new detainee what his motivations were to work with Al Qaeda or one of the other insurgent or terrorist groups, so I could target my approach to his weak points. When I found a man working for monetary gain, then I might ask, "So, now that you are in prison, who is going to support your family?" If that seemed to have an effect, I might offer to write a letter recommending that he be released early if he cooperated.

As I conducted more interrogations, I developed a reputation within the camp as an interrogator who would listen to the detainee's case and could make things happen for them. Sometimes I would have a prisoner moved to a better facility or would arrange for some glowing recommendations or pardons written by our JAG officers. Of course, none of these agreements were legally binding, but they played a big role in obtaining cooperation and building my reputation within the camp.

Many of the interrogators I worked with were too preoccupied with determining their detainee's guilt or involvement with terrorist or insurgent organizations to see the benefit of my methods. This tunnel vision on the issue of culpability was further amplified by our officer in charge, whose background was as a criminal investigator. He would constantly ask us, "Is he guilty?" or "Did he do it?"

The Air Force Office of Special Investigations that he came from was a whole different ball game from the world of HUMINT. Though the Office of Special Investigations did some HUMINT work, they were mostly focused on the criminal aspect and functioned more like the FBI than a true clandestine agency like the CIA or DIA. I wished everyone would understand that the mentality of constantly trying to find out if the detainees were guilty was a flawed way of thinking. In my book, it made for a poor interrogator. It didn't matter if the prisoner was the one at fault or not. What mattered was whether he possessed information of intelligence value and whether I could obtain it.

Shortly after I had made these discoveries, I started a new case that would cement in my mind just how valuable using the correct approach was. I was assigned a local tribal sheik who had been apprehended for suspicion of being an

Al Qaeda leader in one of the larger cities in the Diyala province. He was known as Fatman in the camp—I'm pretty sure it had something to do with the fact that he was five foot six and weighed more than 350 pounds. Knowing that Fatman held a high position in the community, I decided to interrogate him in the comfort booth. Unlike our normal interrogation booths, this comfort booth was a bit more spacious, with two leather chairs, a couch, a hookah pipe, and a TV.

Before he stepped into my booth, I reviewed the dossier on my detainee. Fatman was from the rich farmlands of the Diyala province, near one of the larger and more diversified cities in the region. He had a wife and five children, two daughters and three sons. A lot of what I read in the file didn't surprise me, but the details of his capture caught my attention.

It had been about 0200 hours when five Humvees loaded down with a Special Operation team had approached his farmhouse. They had stopped the vehicles a few hundred meters away from the perimeter of his property and proceeded on foot to the house. After quickly checking the outlying buildings, they had surrounded the house and positioned several breach teams at the entrances into the house. Without giving away their presence, they had launched a sudden coordinated assault on all of the doors and quickly swept the house to identify the target of the raid.

Without incident, all of the other members of the household had been peacefully subdued. No shots had been fired, and no one had been killed. Fatman had been swiftly ushered away into custody and escorted into one of the Humvees that was at the ready. Now, two days later, this man was at Camp Cropper and seated on a couch next to me.

As I began my assessment of him, I quickly found that he had a deep booming voice and was a great orator. He was middle-aged, maybe forty-two years old. Fatman loved to talk and tell stories about his family and village, so I let him talk. After twenty minutes or so of him talking, I found that he also worked as the head representative for the Iraqi Islamic Party in his particular city. He represented the different farmers in the local area, and because of his position, he proved to have a vast amount of information about several insurgent groups operating in the area.

Slowly, I was able to glean that Fatman might be willing to talk with me if I would be willing to help him out. He told me, "I heard in the camp that an interrogator may be able to get my charges reduced or even dropped."

I replied, "That's true. But if you want me to do that for you, then you need to be willing to talk with me. This is only way it works."

I spent the next thirty minutes trying to persuade him to provide me with information about the insurgents operating in his area, but it seemed like it was going to be a hopeless cause. He didn't believe he had done anything wrong, or that we had any evidence against him. I needed to show him that we did, so I decided to transition to the futility approach. I stepped outside for a moment to cue up my change in tactics.

A polygraph examiner walked back into the room with me, carrying a heavy black case. He spread out a special pad on a seat, which we directed Fatman to sit on. With the help of the guards, the examiner also attached two straps to his chest that would measure any changes in breathing and heart rate. Two more sensors were added to his index fingers in order to gauge any changes in temperature, sweatiness or oxygenation levels. Once the baseline questions were established, I began to interrogate him again. Each time his vitals spiked, I would turn the monitor around and say, "Look, see this here? I can tell you are lying."

Still, Fatman did not budge.

Finally, I showed him the video of him cutting off the heads of five policemen who had also been Shi'a. I was sure that the blood squirting from their corpses would make for a wonderful response in a criminal court. That was when he agreed to cooperate. He knew that the same evidence would be presented to a judge when he went to trial, so he decided to speak up. Fatman knew he was guilty, and he realized that if he ever wanted to see his family again, he was going to have to cooperate with me. Even though I knew this man had beheaded five people and that several Americans had been killed by a roadside bomb traced back to his farm, I still had to interrogate him and assess him for intelligence value.

As we talked, he admitted, "I know that I'm caught. I want to cooperate...in return, I would like your assurance that you will recommend me for a reduced sentence."

I replied, "I'll agree to this request, but only if you provide me with valuable information."

Fatman said, "I can supply you with the location of a Jaysh al Mahdi battalion commander, as well as a vast number of JAM members, weapon locations, torture houses, and weapon smuggling points from Iran along with the names of Iranians who are working with the JAM commander." Then he proceeded to describe all of these facts in great and gruesome detail.

I asked, "How do you know all this information?"

He just smiled with a devilish look in his eyes and said, "I have my sources."

Knowing that he was a high-level AQI leader, I had no doubt that he did have his own sources. I told him, "I will check on your information. If you are lying to me, it will not go well for you."

Fatman assured me, "My information is accurate." So for the moment, I took him at his word and left to write up my intelligence reports for the field units to act on.

He did, in fact, provide us with the location of a JAM headquarters and a meeting location that we previously hadn't known existed. The location was also being used as a torture house; the JAM members would keep their Sunni prisoners hostage there until a family member paid a ransom, though in most cases, they would kill them. Several days after my report was published, the location was raided, and Coalition Forces or CF found the remains of several tormented victims along with numerous JAM members, which was exactly what Fatman had said we would find.

Fatman also provided us with the site of a rather large weapon cache just outside of town, in a small cluster of houses owned by a Shi'a family. The four brothers used one of the houses as a meeting location once a week to plan and organize attacks on Coalition Forces. Across the street from the house was another big compound with a large single home and two outlying homes. The man who owned that home was responsible for smuggling weapons from Iran to this particular area to be used by JAM in their attacks against the Sunnis and CF. A Special Forces team raided the location and found large amounts of weapons, IEDs, and explosively formed penetrators, or EFPs, from Iran, as well as numerous other weapons.

Fatman wasn't willing to betray his own organization, and it would have been pointless to talk to him about it. However, he was more than happy to provide information about his enemies. Most interrogators would have gotten frustrated and written this case off and moved on. However, if they had done that, they would have failed to realize the other information of intelligence value that could have been collected.

There is an old and true adage, *The enemy of my enemy is my friend.* I realized that this AQI leader was just using US forces to eliminate his enemies, but so what? There were standing orders to find any and all information regarding AQI, but the same was true of JAM and any Iranian involvement, of which there was a lot, despite what the government was saying publicly. In this case, I simply had to think outside of the box to find the information, which likely saved a lot of innocent civilians' and US soldiers' lives by removing those weapons and eliminating one smuggling route.

The risk of conducting raids is high. You know that the objective being hit is going to have weapons and people trained in how to use them. Unfortunately for our side, we lost three Americans in the raids we conducted based on Fatman's information. This was the first time we lost American lives on a mission that I had built. It sounds strange, but I just didn't let myself think about it at the time. It was terrible that three Americans died, and I think about that often even years after the fact, but we also killed or captured over two dozen of the enemy and disrupted a major JAM network in the area. With the announcement of the coming troop surge, we would all have to get used to taking losses with the successes.

Chapter 4
The Holidays in the Desert

Soon after the raids based on the intelligence from Fatman, it came time for Christmas. Thankfully, dinner that night was much better than our Thanksgiving dinner had been, so at least the evening started out on a good stomach. As a Christmas gift, our unit also had a bathroom trailer installed near our building. This may not sound like a big deal, but going to the bathroom using a real toilet, even one that got clogged half the time, was far better than having to use one of those nasty porta-johns. Porta-johns either ran out of toilet paper, leaving us to make some sort of alternate arrangement, or they stank to high heaven. And then, of course, there was the "hover factor." No one wanted to make a splash with the dirty, nasty chemical water that everyone had been relieving themselves in, so to avoid ruining the rest of the day, we all learned to hover. So obviously, this particular Christmas present was definitely much appreciated.

Although it was Christmas and to many of us it was a holy day, there was still work to be done and our management said we had to work through the holiday. Interrogating a terrorist was a pretty lousy way to spend Christmas, but one that I will never forget. So, to lighten the mood for myself and my interpreter, I chose to do a rather unconventional interrogation.

I chose to read the Christmas story to my detainee and drink some hot chocolate with him. I gave him a piece of paper and allowed him to write a letter home. He asked me, "Why are you giving me hot chocolate, and why are you reading to me from the Bible?"

I explained to him, "Today is Christmas. It is our holy day, and just as you Muslims talk to me about Allah during Ramadan, I am talking to you about Christ on Christmas." The detainee didn't particularly care one way or the other. He wasn't offended by me reading to him; he was just thankful for the hot chocolate and the chance to write a letter home.

My family back home had gone to the pastor of their church and organized several large shipments of Christmas presents to be sent to the troops. The packages arrived a couple of days after Christmas, but when they came, they came in force. I received fifty-six packages, with each of them containing between two and three individually wrapped presents. I was a rather popular guy for the next week as I passed out Christmas presents to everyone in my unit. It felt good to get something at Christmas; it helped to remind us that though we were far away, we were not forgotten. My wife's aunt, who works for Ghirardelli Chocolate in San

Francisco, also sent me twenty pounds of chocolate—that's a lot of chocolate bars to hand out.

Christmas was also a tough time for those of us living on Camp Stryker. We nearly lost one of our interrogators during a mission. Inside our unit was a small group that consisted of two interrogators and analysts whose sole focus was to find the body of SSG Keith "Matt" Maupin, who had been captured by AQI forces on April 9, 2004. Despite a video that had surfaced, showing him being executed and dumped into a shallow grave, we hadn't found the body and burial site. The military has a long-standing tradition of not leaving a man behind, even if he is killed. This team had received a tip about a possible location of the body, so just prior to Christmas, they had left with a platoon of engineers who knew how to run a backhoe and a company of infantry for security.

While on site, they suddenly began to take mortar and RPG fire. Within an instant, heavy machine guns were also shooting at them. The soldier operating the backhoe was hit. A bullet went through the side of his body armor, and he slowly bled to death. Another soldier who had been manning one of the machine guns of another vehicle had his arm shot off—fortunately, he survived the wound. Eventually, the attackers were killed as the infantrymen encircled the location that the machine-gun fire was coming from and a couple of gunships overhead made sure no one else escaped. Fortunately, the interrogators from our group that had been on site were fine, other than being shaken up by the events.

Meanwhile, the death toll among the civilian population in Iraq was skyrocketing out of control. There were reports of hundreds of people being killed a week, and sometimes a day, by JAM death squads and AQI, specifically targeting Shi'a neighborhoods and marketplaces. JAM was particularly known for stopping traffic in Sunni neighborhoods, pulling people out of their cars and executing them on the spot. Sometimes they would go through all the houses in a particular block and pull all the men and boys into the streets before they would make a spectacle of cutting their heads off in front of their families. This would then be followed by the Sunnis and/or AQI going to a Shi'a-controlled area and repeating the process. If something wasn't done quickly, the country was quickly going to be torn apart as religious and ethnic cleansing would only intensify. Our hope was that, with the addition of these 30,000 combat troops, we would be able to crush the insurgency and allow the government time to mature and stabilize.

Unfortunately, the surge had a direct negative impact on my life personally. I went from having one roommate to two—that made three of us in a twelve-foot-by-twelve-foot square, all on different schedules. As I was supposed to be sleeping, both of my roommates would have to be coming in or leaving on opposite shifts. My new roommate was also one of those guys that hits the snooze button *several* times before getting up. I felt like I had a newborn baby living in my room with the number of times I was woken up at night, even with the use of Ambien.

Somehow, I would drag myself out of bed every day, throw on my shorts and flip-flops and hoist myself into the shower to try and wake myself up. The cold night air usually would do the trick, as it got down to the forties during the winter. Then I would grab some food from the DFAC, trudge on over to ICE, code and badge myself in to where I would eat at my desk while checking my secure emails. Then it was a twelve-to-sixteen-hour day, every day, with no days off. Sometimes, I wouldn't have time to go to lunch or midnight chow. Fortunately, the guys were pretty good about grabbing food for you if you asked. Before I knew it, my shift would be over, and I would be headed back to my POD. Wash, rinse repeat, each day much the same as the day before.

One way or another, I hadn't really gotten along with a lot of my fellow interrogators. Some of it may have been my fault, since I do have a very direct personality. I'm not sure if I said something wrong during training, but I didn't really have a lot of friends, except for a few of the contractors that were there and my original roommate. In some ways, it was good that things were so busy. It didn't allow me to ruminate on my loneliness very much.

During the downtime that I did have, I would try to watch TV shows or movies on my computer. I needed to escape from the life I was in, and to think about anything but these horrible terrorist acts and the despicable people I spent my days talking with. Other times, I would go for walks around the perimeter to clear my head and, in my better moments, pray.
****

Shortly after Christmas, the New Year quickly approached, and with it came a lot of uncertainty about the time left on our deployment. On New Year's Eve, I was sitting in the ICE, chewing the fat with a few friends, when suddenly the camp alarm system went off. Within seconds, an NCO from the operations room came running in and yelled, "Grab your body armor and go man your battle stations! *Now!*"

As it turned out, the prisoners in the camp had decided to throw their own New Year's Eve party in the form of a riot and prison break. I quickly donned my body armor and grabbed my gas mask. All of the contingency training kicked in, and I sped along on autopilot. I was getting ready to move out when the ops officer barked, "No, leave your rifle! Grab a squad automatic weapon and some ammo!"

As I was getting the weapon and ammo, I was told to head out with two other interrogators to a guard tower on the southern end of the camp. As we ran, I heard someone yell, "Shoot any escaping prisoners if they show up near your tower!"

As I picked up speed, I thought to myself, *Wow. I've trained for this, but this is really the first time I might actually have to shoot someone.* I wasn't sure what to make of that, but I didn't have time to dwell on it.

The three of us made it to our battle position fairly quickly and climbed up into the guard tower. I positioned the machine gun to face toward the camp and any possible escape routes that a prisoner might try to take if he were to come our way. Once our position was set up and secure, we just stood there and watched in awe as the prison guards completely blanketed the entire camp in tear gas. The low-lying white clouds were supposed to help gain some sort of control in the camp, but it was obvious that the tear gas wasn't going to do the trick on its own.

Shots rang out as the guards started firing rubber bullets at several prisoners who had broken through the first fence. I felt like I was watching something out of a war movie—but this was very real. Some of the guards started throwing "donkey balls," which were essentially modified grenades—when one explodes, it scatters tiny rubber balls in every direction, stunning those who get hit. To further add to the mayhem, someone shot off several red flares over the exterior of the prison to ensure our lines of sight were well lit up. The cacophony of rubber bullets being fired, donkey balls exploding and flares being shot into the air, along with all the smoke from the tear gas and flashbangs, made for a surreal experience as the scene continued to unfold for close to an hour.

Within the first five minutes after the alarm sounded, several hundred military police soldiers swarmed out of their barracks to the prison in an attempt to regain control and subdue the prisoners. Some of the guards were running with nothing on other than their boxers, boots, body armor and their rifles. Fortunately for us, no prisoners broke through the second layer of defense or got near our guard tower. However, we did have to stand guard for several more hours and endure a few strong whiffs of tear gas as the wind changed directions.

We found out later that evening that half a dozen prisoners had somehow cut a hole in the fence that encased them and used the distraction of the riot to try to escape. They hadn't accounted for how they were going to get past the second layer of fencing that also encircled the camp, or the numerous guards that would surely be manning the catwalks during an escape. In the end, no prisoners had fled the grasp of the camp, and no detainees had died. Several men were injured in the evening's event, and it was definitely not the way I wanted to be spending my holiday.

The following day at the DFAC, Camp Cropper was the talk of the town. Word had spread quickly across the Victory Base Complex, or VBC, about the massive prison riot at Camp Cropper. Of course, it didn't help that multiple bases that are part of the VBC complex dispatched their quick reaction forces to surround our camp in case a prisoner was able to make it past all of the guards and defenses. Typically, one gets used to hearing the occasional shots fired near or around VBC, but the commotion that had ensued from our little adventure had woken up the entire complex. With the tumultuous din of several thousand rounds being fired, dozens of donkey balls and flashbangs exploding, and the whoosh of flares lighting up the night sky, everyone in the VBC became concerned that one of the perimeters had been breached. I suppose it was good to know that we had probably close to 3,000 soldiers and armored vehicles surrounding our camp in case things got really out of control.

Chapter 5
Breaking the Back of Ansar al Sunnah

God had been good to me my first few months in Iraq, and I firmly believe that I was having the success I was because I had prayed about each case. I asked God what to say to each detainee to get him to open up, and up to this point, it had worked. Now I was going to be pitted against a more formidable challenge: this method of interrogation that I had developed was going to be put to the test.

Shortly after completing Fatman's case, I was once again provided with the opportunity to take a shot at a tough nut that the DIA and CIA interrogators hadn't been able to crack up to this point. Majid was a particularly uncooperative detainee, and after several months, the various agencies gave up on getting any useful information from him, opting to focus their attention on someone else instead. Everyone knew that Majid was a high-ranking member of the Ansar al Sunnah organization, and most were content with just having him detained.

Although I had only been interrogating for a couple of months, I already understood that, though these detainees were terrorists, they were still human beings. They still had hopes, dreams, families, and the same desires you would expect a normal person to have. I became adept at using these chinks in their armor against them to get at what I was after. The first day after I was handed Majid's case, I spent some time looking at the previous interrogators' notes. I realized that they had taken a very harsh approach with him, using some tactics and techniques that we military interrogators were not allowed to use. I also read Majid's background and discovered that he had a degree in economics from the University of Baghdad. Economics was one of my favorite courses of study in college. I had considered pursuing a degree in that subject myself. I concluded that this would be a good common point of interest to begin our conversation with.

During the first meeting, I brought Majid into the comfort booth. He seemed surprised by the surroundings as he slowly sat in the accommodating leather chair. I brought in some hot tea and began my assessment of this rather short, skinny man. We spent the first twenty minutes getting to know each other and just enjoying our tea. I asked him numerous questions about college and his degree in economics.

Majid told me, "I wanted to go into business and run my own company. I loved the world of economics and believed that I could leverage that passion into a prosperous business."

We spent the next hour talking about finances, globalization, and numerous other topics. At the end of the interrogation, I told him, "I enjoyed our conversation." Then I asked, "What is your favorite food?"

I could tell he was skeptical at first as his eyebrow rose in a questioning manner. However, after a little more pleasant conversation, he responded, "I really enjoy roasted chicken."

I replied, "We'll meet again in a couple of days and have dinner together. I will also bring you a cell phone and allow you to talk with your wife."

His eyes lit up—at this point, he had not seen or spoken with his wife in almost three months. He shook my hand and thanked me.

A couple of days later we met, and as I promised, we had dinner together. I brought him an herb-roasted chicken with a salad, cucumbers, olives and some fresh fruit. My interpreter had told me that most Arabs love cucumbers and olives, so I made sure to include plenty of those with his meal. Majid enjoyed it immensely, smiling like a man who had just seen his first sunrise.

After we finished eating, I brought out the cell phone and allowed him to talk to his wife for about ten minutes. When he'd had a moment to reflect on his conversation, I just asked him point-blank, "Why are you in the camp, Majid?"

He replied, "I am here because I am a member of Ansar al Sunnah."

"I know that," I said, "but who are you in the organization?"

He smiled and then laughed and said, "You don't know?"

"No, I don't know," I replied, playing stupid.

Up to this point, we assumed, based on intelligence, that we knew his position in Ansar al Sunnah, but he hadn't confirmed it. I needed to know if we were right. Majid sat back in his chair and casually said, "I am the General Emir of Western Iraq. I am number three in the organization."

I nearly fell out of my chair when he confirmed this to me while I tried to maintain a neutral façade. It took me only a second to ask him, "Why are you willing to tell me this, even though you didn't mention it to the previous interrogators?"

He simply said, "You are the first interrogator to treat me like a human being, and I like you."

Too often, interrogators treated their detainees with disdain and disrespect; this led to a great deal of animosity. However, friendliness and likeability are essential traits of effective interrogators, just as they are essential in business. It's also good to keep in mind that only a fine line separates them from us. If they had invaded our country, then we could be the prisoners and they would be the interrogators. I think if you can look at things from this perspective, you are already far ahead of many interrogators.

Now that Majid had told me who he was and what his role was in the organization, I probed a little further. "Would you be willing to talk with me about the organization as a whole?" I made it clear that I was not out to make a case against him. I simply wanted to understand his organization.

Majid was a relatively small man. He also had an ego that had been seriously beaten down, and I could tell from the three hours I'd spent with him that he could use a boost in his self-worth and sense of importance. I saw this weakness and exploited it by taking on a more deferential and quizzical approach, allowing him to feel like the smart one in the room. Leveraging this adjusted approach, I said to Majid, "Since you're among the highest-ranking members of your organization, you would be able to speak with the Americans almost like an ambassador from your organization, allowing for more open dialogue."

Despite him being a prisoner, Majid now had the sense that he was the most important person in the camp, and this was his opportunity to brag about his organization. Majid went for the bait and explained, "I want to help clarify several misconceptions about my organization and Al Qaeda in Iraq."

I barely managed to cover up my excitement. This particular piece of information was extremely high in value and was a top priority to obtain because there were rumors of the two organizations possibly merging.

Majid said, "Ansar al Sunnah is primarily focused on attacking you Americans. We do not agree with AQI's indiscriminate attacks against civilians and fellow Muslims. We only wanted to kill Americans. Al Qaeda wants to attack the Iraqi government, the Shi'a *and* the Americans." AQI had been working hard to unify the Sunnis against the Shi'a-led government; however, their wide-ranging attacks, which had also killed a lot of Sunnis, were having an adverse effect on their ambitions.

With ease, Majid talked about the entire breakdown of his organization. He proudly explained who was in charge of the different provinces in Iraq and the operational structure of the organization, which he had proudly built into a force that was beating the Americans. One of the most important pieces of information Majid provided was how the senior leadership of the organization was able to elude coalition capture. The military head of the organization, Karem, the number two in the organization, had been previously detained by Coalition Forces and released in the winter of 2005. While being detained, he had observed the US military and our organizational structure and had determined that if he were released, he would reorganize his organization to resemble ours. After his discharge from the camp, he reshaped his insurgent organization, making it difficult for us to identify the senior leadership. To this day, I still cannot believe we let this guy go.

I was absolutely amazed at how much information Majid knew and at his willingness to talk. He wanted to show off his organization, and I used his ego and pride to get him to disclose more than he probably would have otherwise. He gladly explained to me, "One of the reasons you were unsuccessful in capturing our senior leadership is because of the compartmentalization of the organization. Each zone or region in Iraq has been given a general emir who is in charge of the entire region; each general emir has a military emir and a media emir."

A wry smile formed on his lips, and then he continued, "Neither the military emir nor the media emir know each other or have any contact with each other. The military emir and the media emir also have their own commanders, who in turn never know who the general emir is."

As he continued to talk with me, his tone changed from one of trepidation to one of disdain and strength. He was talking down to me while bragging about how smart his group was and how stupid we Americans were. I continued to play into this by praising him and his organization for how well they had done at beating the great Americans, saying that we had a lot to learn from his group. He'd just smile and nod, as if I had converted to his cause. He didn't realize that he had fallen into a well-planned trap I had guided him into, or how much intelligence he was unknowingly giving away. Earlier in our training at Fort Huachuca, I remembered one of my instructors giving me that example of a detainee giving you a tour of the rooms in his home, and being ready with questions to exploit it. Majid was giving me the grand tour of his mental house.

I continued to bring Majid meals from our DFAC, so he was eating the good stuff. Then we would sip on some chai, and as he puffed away on the hookah pipe, he continued to talk further. He gave a great explanation of how this level of compartmentalization and removal from the leadership greatly insulated the organization, making it difficult to identify the senior leaders.

Majid quickly became my golden goose of information. He unwittingly gave all the names of the senior general emirs in the organization and the regional breakdown of the organization, such as who was in charge of which area. Unfortunately, he didn't know who their military emirs were because of the compartmentalization. However, he had met all the general emirs and was able to provide us with a great deal of biographical information on all of them, including the locations of each of their previous meetings.

While Majid was unsuspectingly giving away intelligence, he also explained what had happened in the pivotal meetings between the senior leadership of Ansar al Sunnah and Al Qaeda. Majid wanted me to know that he had several problems with Al Qaeda. "I do not approve of their blanket suicide bombing attacks—innocent people were killed. My group would never do that," he said.

He continued to explain, "My group had several run-ins with the AQI groups in my area because of our disagreement. These problems nearly spiraled into a full-scale battle between AQI and Ansar al Sunnah in the Al Anbar province—that is, until the senior leaders of both organizations met to discuss their differences."

I learned how, in the fall of 2006, the senior leader of Ansar al Sunnah had held a personal meeting with a senior leader of AQI to decide what future the two organizations might have of either fighting together or coordinating attacks. This information about a meeting between Karem and a senior AQI leader was particularly significant. Up to this point, the Coalition Forces had no idea that the senior leaders of both organizations had actually held formal talks about their growing disagreement and future plans.

Shortly after I published my report about this meeting, I was bombarded with several source-directed requests from the central fusion analysis cell in Baghdad that filters all the intelligence gathered in Iraq to try and piece together a bigger picture of what's going on in the country. Everyone wanted more information. I was asked to give a briefing to several senior military leaders and advisors.

After further conversations with Majid, I was able to learn the location of the meeting place and was able to get his point of view on a possible merger between the two organizations. Majid boldly stated, "I would sooner leave the organization or start my own than merge with AQI. I have philosophical disagreements with them."

From his tone of disgust, I could tell that he truly didn't like them, although he was more than willing to use them to further his own organization's goals of removing the Americans from his country.

In total, I obtained twenty IIRs from Majid. These reports became the most complete biographical and operational history of the organization to date. I was later told that the information I produced helped to shape several new tactical shifts in targeting Ansar al Sunnah, which later in my tour proved to be the turning point in the near annihilation of this particular insurgent organization.

Majid's was the largest case I had handled up to this point. It proved to be pivotal in setting me apart from my peers as a top interrogator. Oddly enough, I was still juggling seven other cases while handling Majid's. And despite the success I was having, I was dealing with an immense amount of flak from my tiger team partner, my analyst.

****

Conducting interrogations can be extremely time-consuming. A smart interrogator will study the capture package in the detainee's electronic folder, any intelligence reporting discussing him, and related information about his group and their activities in the area he was operating in. This tertiary information is important as it helps you develop a larger picture before talking with the detainee. This is where the concept of introducing the analyst to work as a partnered team member with an interrogator was born. A good analyst will build an overview of your area of responsibility, what groups are in it, who leads them and so on. This way the interrogations can be more specific and targeted. A typical interrogation time slot was two hours. An interrogator could schedule his interrogation for up to twenty-three hours of the day with one detainee, but most interrogations lasted under the two-hour mark. Maximizing one's time was critical as we typically handled between eight and eighteen detainees at one time. With four time slots a day, you had to pick and choose who would get most of your time and effort.

Upon my arrival into Iraq, I was assigned a young, idealistic and very opinionated analyst. Let's just say she was not who I had hoped to have on my tiger team. She was a great person and very good at her job, but our personalities just didn't pair well. The interrogator is supposed to be the driver, and the analyst is the navigator—my problem was she wanted to do both, and she was very obstinate about it. When she didn't get her way or agree with me, she would openly challenge me, attempting to make a public scene so as to get me to capitulate to her demands as opposed to finding a compromise we could agree on or just following my lead as the interrogator. However, being a somewhat astute interrogator, I saw exactly what she was trying to do, and I was not about to be manipulated by these petty antics. Regardless, this internal conflict caused me an extreme amount of grief and was very distracting. It seemed that for every success I had, there was always a corresponding struggle or two.

In the end, after numerous requests, I was finally assigned a new analyst. My new analyst, Jeremy, was far and away the most competent and professional analyst I had worked with. He came from a small town in Oklahoma and was a member of the Air Force Reserves, though he was working in Iraq as a contractor when he was assigned to work with me. It wasn't his first rodeo either. He'd already served a four-month tour in Iraq and had previous experience working in the human intelligence field. The man was a technological wizard as well.

Jeremy would begin every day by scanning through the list of incoming detainees from the other forward operating bases and missions. Before they even went through the initial screening interview, he would identify which prisoners came from our region of interest and organize them by the specific village they were from. Then he plotted all of the information on a very organized Excel spreadsheet he had created. Using his data, we could quickly identify inbound detainees who might have a tie to some of our existing cases. Within a week of using Jeremy's system and putting in requests to interview specific detainees, we had already tracked down several men who were involved in our ongoing targeting mission. The goal wasn't to find a "Golden Detainee" who would just spew out information for months. We wanted to locate a piece of the puzzle here and another one there, until we had formed a clear picture of what was going on. If we found another golden goose like Fatman or Majid along the way, all the better.

Going from an analyst who constantly disagreed with me to one that anticipated my moves and was always one step ahead of me was a completely different world. Jeremy quickly became an absolutely invaluable team member and eventually became a good friend. Having lost the constant friction, my job became easier. However, the coming months would prove to be a trying period for us both. We were about to be handed one of the most important cases we would interrogate during our time in Iraq.

Chapter 6
False Flags and a Helicopter Ride

The story of this interrogation comes from my roommate, Red, who gave me permission to share it after having written down a lot of details for me. Red was assigned to Combined Joint Special Operations Task Forces—Central, which was located not too far from our own base. They conducted a raid on an embassy in the north of Iraq, arresting several men of the Iranian Revolutionary Guard Council, or IRGC, that were planted to help smuggle foreign fighters over the border into Iraq. These men were literally hours from receiving their diplomatic papers, which would mean automatic immunity, even if they were guilty. The task force had to act now or never. Interrogators for this group were hand-selected by the task force operators, and Red was one of the chosen.

The abduction took place early in the morning, between 0100 and 0300. The men were snatched in the darkness, with bags being pulled over their heads before they were thrown in the back of the truck. While they were still reeling from the shock of capture, frightened and disoriented, they were questioned in the vehicle while en route to a special remote prison. However, after several days of conventional interrogations, neither the task force guys nor Red and his partner were getting anywhere, so Red proposed that they try and pull a false flag on these detainees. Since one of them was the religious leader of the lot and was supposed to keep the others on task by reporting their actions back to ████████████, he would have to be the one we broke. If we could break him, then the others would follow like sheep.

Knowing the "deep love" shared between the Israeli Mossad and the IRGC, Red learned that one of the SF guys could speak Arabic with a Hebrew accent and talked him into joining this little ruse. A plan was hatched, and the proposal was approved through the appropriate channels.

With the stage set behind the scenes, Red confidently walked into the interrogation booth and announced to the detainee, "Well, things are very simple. If you won't talk to me, then you are going to be transferred to another camp, one that isn't run by US forces. You will have to deal with a whole new set of interrogators."

The prisoner spat at Red's feet and turned his head away in disgust.

The guards placed the eye shade, earmuffs and hood on the prisoner and led him to a helicopter. They all loaded into the chopper and flew in circles around Baghdad for hours, making the prisoner believe he was being flown to an entirely new location that was far, far away.

When they landed, they brought the prisoner to a poorly lit room with black walls and placed him in a metal chair. A light was hanging from the ceiling over his head. It was meant to be the menacing interrogation scene from the old noir movies.

Red asked the prisoner, "One last time, would you like to answer my questions now, or be handed over?"

The prisoner said nothing. The game was afoot.

Red nodded to a man standing in the corner, just outside the light. "He's all yours," he announced. Turning back to the prisoner, he shook his head and said, "You should have chosen to talk to me."

As the task force soldier stepped into the light, the prisoner saw the Mossad uniform he was wearing as he greeted the prisoner in Arabic with a Hebrew accent. "*Ah Salam Alakem, Habibi*," he said.

Nothing else was said. At this point, the Iranian evacuated his bowels—literally—and was pleading to talk with Red. In English, he shouted out, "I will answer any question, just do not hand me over to the Mossad!"

At this point, Red nodded to the SF soldier imitating the Mossad, and he left the room. The Iranian proceeded to tell Red everything he wanted to know and then some. He was very motivated to keep himself from being handed over to the Mossad.

This was an elaborate ruse that required a lot of coordination and approvals, but it was highly effective. Later on, I would have the opportunity to use the technique myself.

Chapter 7
The Surge and a Downed F-15

As January of 2007 drew to a close, we sat around listening to President Bush announce a massive troop surge during his State of the Union address. In the ICE, we talked amongst ourselves about what this surge would mean and if this just might be the thing we needed to turn things around in Iraq. Little did we know that Camp Stryker, the base we were housed at, was about to become one of the major camps used to help facilitate this surge. When we had arrived in Iraq, our camp had around 3,500 people living in it, but as the additional troops continued to arrive into Iraq, our camp swelled to nearly 11,000 soldiers and their vehicles. Unlike support troops, these new troops were all brigade combat teams with one mission—kill the insurgency.

Toward the end of January, we changed one of our interrogation booths from what had been coined "the discomfort room." The room was a larger interrogation room with just a couple of chairs and extremely disturbing images on the walls. The walls were covered from floor to ceiling with images of people shot, blown apart, and beheaded and children ripped to shreds by IEDs, being carried by their crying parents. The intent of the room was to show up close and personal the consequences of the detainees' actions and the pain and anguish they were causing their fellow Iraqis and Muslims.

This room was marginally effective against the detainees. However, it was also having an adverse effect on us interrogators. Several of us interrogators complained about having to store our IBA in this room, or having to use this room at all, because we didn't want to see these images ourselves on a regular basis. The detainee might see these images once during an interrogation, but we might have to see these images over and over. The pictures of the torn-apart children and the mangled bodies were at times just too much to bear, even for us interrogators. After enough interrogators complained about it, our management agreed to take down the images, and we turned the room into a regular interrogation room for future use. There are some images no one should have to see, let alone on a regular basis.

As January gave way to February and March, the Joint Intelligence and Debriefing Center, or JIDC, went through a very troubling time. Mike, one of my fellow Air Force interrogators, was questioning a particularly tough detainee. The man had hidden the body of an American pilot whose F-15 had crashed on his farm in the Al Anbar province. The prisoner was not exactly cooperative, and as time continued to pass without our locating the body, tension built. Given the gravity of the situation, Mike decided to use some tougher interrogation tactics, which still fell within the guidelines of the regulation and the law of course.

For some unexplainable reason, his analyst decided that it would be funny to write a dialogue of the interrogation adding salacious details of things that hadn't happened to sensationalize it for some of her friends who were stationed at another base in Iraq. In her email, she said the detainee had been placed in various stress positions, denied water and physically threatened to be burned with a cigarette. His analyst was apparently bored and wanted to impress her friends. The problem was she exaggerated what had actually happened to make it a more impressive story. She sent this email to her friend, who then forwarded it to a couple more friends and so on. Before long, the dialogue of the interrogation—complete with all the parts that were incorrect and sensationalized—had been sent to several dozen people and an official complaint was forwarded to our task force commander, stating, "This interrogation appears to be similar to the stuff that went on at Abu Ghraib."

I know beyond a doubt that what went on during that interrogation didn't violate any regulations or laws, because I saw the interrogation on video while it was being conducted. I saw the prisoner after the interrogation with my own eyes, and he had not been tortured or kept in any stress positions. However, because of what had been sent out in the email and because a complaint had been lodged, a formal investigation was launched. Mike was pulled from interrogating prisoners and only allowed to monitor them while the investigation was conducted, which lasted about two weeks. In the end, it was determined that there was no wrongdoing and Mike was cleared—or so we thought.

While the Army commanders who we all worked for dismissed the complaint after reviewing the video evidence, the complaint still had to go through the Air Force administrative group in Balad. The command element there decided that while Mike had not specifically broken any laws during his interrogation, the entire incident was an embarrassment to the Air Force. Therefore, they had Mike sent to Balad, where he received an Article 15 for "conduct unbecoming the Air Force." Although it was basically a phony charge, Mike was still sent home. Upon arriving back at his home station, the Article 15 was overturned, and he was given back his rank and was even promoted the following year. Mike was an outstanding airman, and our administrative leadership in Balad had no clue about our mission or what we were doing. They were quick to see slights where they didn't exist and come down hard on those they thought embarrassed their command.

The whole incident was a severe blow to our morale. All of us interrogators were on edge; we had felt and now knew that our Air Force leadership wasn't going to support us or back us up, which unfortunately turned out to be true in more ways than one.

Chapter 8
Camp Bucca Madness

Around the same time, another incident happened with our interrogation detachment down at Camp Bucca that added insult to injury. A couple of the NCOs at Bucca had noticed that there was a security problem with one of the fences near the compound where they worked. This gap in between a fence and a gate could allow a detainee to escape or gain access to their secured location. Although they brought the issue to the guards' attention numerous times, nothing was done to address the security threat.

After a while, one of them got the idea to illustrate the problem with the fence by putting on a yellow jumpsuit and dressing up like a detainee. He and another junior NCO were soon wandering around in the restricted area, looking like a couple of escaped prisoners. Maybe it seemed to them like an innocent thing to do, but pretty soon, one of the guards in the watchtower noticed what he thought were two detainees roving around in a restricted area. He did exactly what he was trained to do and immediately sounded the alarm for escaping prisoners. This also sent out the call for the base's quick reaction force to go and round them up.

Once the two NCOs saw that the guards didn't recognize that they were Americans, they immediately took off the jumpsuits to show the guards that they were wearing American uniforms. However, by the time the guards realized that the two men were not prisoners trying to escape, it was too late to call off the base's reaction force or stand down the base-wide alert. The situation caused the entire base to go into immediate lockdown and set off an entire chain of events, including an alert being sent to Task Force 134 Command in Baghdad that the base had a prison break. This also immediately put several additional units on alert to fly down to Bucca to assist in recovering detainees if needed.

Fortunately, in the end, no one was hurt, but the two NCOs were in some serious hot water. Both of them had to explain to the military police commander and the base commander exactly what they had been doing and why. At first, the Army command element in Baghdad was content with giving them both a letter of reprimand and letting things end at that. Unfortunately for us, our Air Force commander in Balad didn't think the situation had been dealt with firmly enough, and he had them flown to Balad while he figured out what he wanted to do with them. After two weeks, both were given an Article 15 for "conduct unbecoming the Air Force" and were then sent home.

So, within a span of three weeks, our Air Force command element in Balad had sent three of our forty-eight NCOs home for arguable charges. Aside from destroying unit morale, this significantly diminished our interrogating capabilities. Each of the interrogators could have conducted approximately 350 interrogations in a year, which meant a loss of 1,050 interrogations. Who knows what information might have been identified or how many lives might have been saved by uncovering that information, not to mention the twenty-eight weeks of training that had been invested in them prior to our deployment to Iraq? In my personal opinion, the leadership in Balad should not have sent these people home. The end result was that the overall mission was hurt while nothing of value was gained in return.

Despite all this drama that was unfolding in our unit, I still had cases to maintain and detainees to interrogate. Even though there was a growing sense that any mistake could get you sent home, I had to at least pretend to go on with life as usual.

Chapter 9
The Monster that was 007

We were now about four months into our deployment—four months of twelve-to-sixteen-hour days, every day, with no days off. It was at this point that the Special Forces Task Force came back to ask for ten more guys to add to their team. All of the guys who had previously volunteered were now burnt out, tired, disillusioned and maybe a little jaded—including myself. None of us wanted to go work even more hours at that point, for any reason. When no one put their hand up to volunteer this time around, Command was not very happy.

The task force decided they would take all of the previous volunteers and interview them to find the men to fill their holes. Some of the guys purposely answered questions wrong, just so that they wouldn't be assigned to the Special Forces unit.

I overheard them ask one of the master sergeants, "What would you do to get a prisoner talking?"

You could tell he kind of leaned in before responding, "*Whatever it takes.*"

Another guy was asked, "Would you abuse a prisoner?" To which he replied, "Only if they had it coming."

It was like watching a bunch of people trying to say something inappropriate in order to get out of jury duty.

When they got to me, they asked me a more direct question, so I was able to give a more direct answer. They asked, "Do you want to join the Special Forces Task Force?"

"No," was my honest answer.

"Why not?" they queried.

"I'm already tired out of my mind working twelve-to-sixteen-hour days, and you want me to work eighteen hours a day? I'm stressed and I'm worn out. Plus, you can't guarantee me that I'll be able to take my midtour and go home to see my wife in a couple of months. Why in the world would I possibly want to work with you?"

They gave me some long, drawn-out explanation about being a part of a larger mission, serving a greater cause...I tuned it out, honestly. It made no difference.

"Look, no offense, but none of that matters to me now. Unless you can guarantee me a midtour and a schedule that's at the very least no more strenuous than my current one, I'm not interested. I already feel that I'm making a difference and a contribution here—I feel no need to further drain myself."

They did not fill their slots.

****

Within a week of concluding Majid's case, I was handed another high-value detainee. I inherited this particular person because he had admitted to being an Ansar al Sunnah leader in the Diyala province—although later we would find out who he was truly working for. Since I was presently the Ansar al Sunnah expert, the case became mine, whether I wanted it or not. I later regretted it being handed to me…this assignment nearly cost me my job as an interrogator and caused me an immense amount of anguish and frustration. However, what he told me thrust me onto the national stage as an interrogator.

The last three digits in the detainee's ID number were, of all things, 007. So I referred to him as 007 from then on. I wasn't sure what to think of this guy the first time I met him. He was a man in his early forties with a medium build, short graying hair, and light brown eyes that appeared very disarming when he smiled. He was well educated, had several degrees, and came from an affluent family. 007 nonchalantly told me, "I was a captain in the former regime, and a member of the Iraqi Intelligence Service."

I was intrigued by his past in the Iraqi equivalent of the CIA, but there was just something about this man that bothered me. Although I had just met him, he seemed devious, conniving, and evil. Yet there was a mystery about him that caused me to want to learn more. I was fascinated by him, but he was also perhaps the most deranged and sick-minded person I had ever had the displeasure of meeting. This man admitted to killing numerous Americans, shooting down a Blackhawk helicopter, and orchestrating suicide bombings all across the Diyala province. He told me a story about how he had kidnapped a Jaysh al Mahdi leader's son and held him for ransom. Once he had received the ransom, he killed the man's son and had the boy cut up into pieces and sent them back to his father in the trunk of a car. He was a true terrorist in every sense of the word.

During my initial assessment of 007, I just sat back and let him talk. He loved to converse at length about numerous different topics. I immediately remembered what my instructor told me about a prisoner who is ready and willing to talk. I let the man chatter for about half an hour before I told him my initial assessment of him. Then I bluntly jumped in, "—I think you're a liar. You don't know what you're talking about. I don't believe a word you're telling me."

It was priceless. At that moment he just sat back and looked surprised, almost hurt. Then he smiled and asked, "Why did you come to that conclusion?"

I told him, "The information you're telling me about Ansar al Sunnah is false."

He looked perplexed and asked, "How do you know that I am lying?"

I replied, "I'm friends with a senior leader in the organization, and he's working as a source for me." Then I proceeded to tell 007 exactly what was wrong with the information he was telling me.

This tactic was a dangerous one in that I risked seriously offending him. This approach was called the "we know all" approach, which is where you essentially lay all your cards on the table, informing the detainee that you know everything about him or the subject he's talking about. It's highly discouraged as it's nearly impossible to pull off. I was taking a calculated risk that my information was correct. Since I knew that he would have had at least some interrogation resistance training in the Iraqi Intelligence Service, I had to test 007 to see if he truly knew any information of value or if he was just wasting my time. I needed to go out on this limb so I could determine what approaches he might be susceptible to next, and so I could figure out exactly how I was going to exploit him while still getting him to want to cooperate.

Realizing that he had been caught, he smirked and then admitted, "OK, I did feed you some false information…but I was just testing your knowledge to see if I could work with you."

"I am not amused," I replied. I quietly let out a big sigh of relief, trying to hide my satisfaction that this risky approach had worked.

He insisted, "I needed to know I was talking with the right person—a person who could make things happen for me."

So I assured him, "If you provide valuable, verifiable information, there's a great deal that I can do for you. You can ask about me in the camp. Many detainees trust me and know that I am a man of my word." It was true—I could even refer him to the CIA to possibly be used as an outside source if they thought his placement and access was good enough and they felt they could flip him.

He nodded in acknowledgement. Due to time constraints, this was the end of our first of many meetings.

During the second interrogation, 007 and I came to an understanding of sorts, and he agreed to answer my questions in exchange for my efforts to help him obtain a reduced sentence or early release. One of the many ruses that I employed as an interrogator was the use of false memorandums or legal documents. I would routinely sit down with our JAG officers and draft these papers for immunity or reduced sentences in exchange for cooperation and complete disclosure of any and all terrorist activities that the detainee had participated in or knew of. This technique was perfectly allowable under our new Army interrogation manual, and it was one that I used with extreme prejudice. It had also helped me develop a reputation in the camp as a man who could make deals happen if you cooperated with me. I began the conversation with my coined phrase, "So why are you here?"

He told me, "I had been the battalion commander of an Ansar al Sunnah group in the Diyala province. Recently my battalion changed sides. Now I am working with the Al Qaeda group operating in the area."

I was surprised at the change and confronted him about it. He stated very clearly, "Over the last six months, Ansar al Sunnah had a problem with funding. They did not have any money. Al Qaeda, on the other hand, is willing to pay good money for well-trained former military members."

007 proceeded to tell me, "I was a former member of Unit 999 during the mid-1990s. I have many contacts from the organization." I later learned that the battalion he commanded was almost exclusively former military and, of all things, littered with former Republican Guard members such as Saddam Fedayeen, as well as members of the Iraqi Black Ops Unit 999. This was an eye opener. We had very few opportunities to interrogate former Unit 999 members, let alone a cooperative one. My head was swimming with questions. Unit 999 was an extremely secretive Iraqi unit during the Saddam era—it was equivalent to the US Delta Force or some of our CIA black ops teams that "don't exist" or you never hear of. They did a lot of foreign operations and mostly black ops work for Saddam, which meant 007 would have had some exceptional placement and access to some very sensitive former regime information.

The following day when I was interrogating 007, he asked me about his charges, which had been delivered to him earlier in the day. Unfortunately, the Iraqi government would often deliver the formal charges to the prisoners in the camp days or weeks after they had arrived. Sometimes this would cause serious problems because cooperative detainees would suddenly become uncooperative once they learned of the charges they were facing. I had to make sure that didn't happen in this case.

I tried to use the situation to my advantage, assuring him, "I could go to your trial and speak to the prosecutor and judge about the tremendous work you have done for the Coalition Forces, and help convince them to give you a reduced sentence or an early release." Because we were a part of an elite interrogation unit, my overall assessment of a detainee as an interrogator did carry some weight in the Iraqi Criminal Court. In some cases, an interrogator's comments could get a detainee a much shorter sentence, even if he had killed a fellow Iraqi.

Deciding to work with me, 007 said, "I want to confess something to you. I am a high-ranking member of Al Qaeda, higher than I have led you to believe. Would it be possible to get my charges dropped if I provide information of 'high value'?"

"You'd have to know the location of bin Laden for that kind of request," I told him.

He smiled and said, "I have one better."

I replied, "We'll have to see…but if you're lying to me, all bets are off."

He told me, "I was at an Al Qaeda training camp in ████ the previous year."

With the ball in my court, I said, "OK. This is of interest, so let's discuss it."

Then he proceeded to provide me with the location of the camp and what he was doing at the camp…but I sensed he was holding something back. More importantly, I saw that he was beginning to get nervous and uncomfortable. His right hand shook a little bit while he was holding his cigarette. This could mean one of two things: either he was nervous about the information he was giving because he was afraid of something, or he was lying.

007 asked me point-blank, "If I tell you something, will you be able to protect my family?"

"Why would your family need protection?" I countered.

He said, "If anyone found out I had told you about what went on at the camp, Al Qaeda would kill my entire family to make an example of me."

I assured 007, "Everything you say will be strictly confidential, and the only ones who would know what we talked about are the four of us in the room: my analyst, the interpreter, me, and you."

At this point, he finally agreed to tell us about the information he had heard at the training camp. He nonchalantly stated, "Ahmed al-Zawahiri was at the camp." Now this name got my complete attention. I knew exactly who this was— the brother of Aymen al-Zawahiri, who was the right-hand man to bin Laden. I immediately knew that if this character was really at the camp, then we might have stumbled onto some valuable information.

I casually responded, "OK, so tell me about the meeting."

He informed me, "I was at the camp to receive some additional training in sniper operations, bomb building and to attempt to gain further access to Al Qaeda outside of Iraq."

"Why would the greater Al Qaeda organization even allow you into their group?" I asked.

007 responded, "My AQI group has had previous contact with Al Qaeda in Jordan, Syria, Saudi Arabia, and Iran. My being at this training camp and meeting was part of a greater plan. I had also already proven myself to them with my service in Iraq. I am also a former Iraqi Intelligence Service and a Unit 999 operative."

He continued, "There were four men of ███ and ███ ██████ descent who were at the camp discussing a plan they were going to carry out against the US in the not-too-far-off future."

"Tell me more about the plan," I probed. "Who is going to be involved, and how many of them are there? Who are the targets? What is the means of carrying out the attack?"

007 explained, "There are eight men and three women who are going to be running the operation on the ground. Three are ██████ citizens and the other eight are from ██████ and ████████. However, the overall plan of the attack came directly from Aymen al-Zawahiri. The attack is a rather complex assault involving many different factors."

He adjusted to get more comfortable in his chair and then continued, "The attack will be directed against two major cities. It is going to involve several different delivery methods across several targets, hitting them all simultaneously. It will make use of vehicle-borne improvised explosive devices and suicide bombers."

This was something we had not yet seen on US soil. My first impression after hearing this information was that it had to be a joke. No one could pull off an attack like this in our own country—but this was the very type of thinking that had allowed the September 11 attacks to happen.

One of the most incredible parts about the attack preparation was how the terrorists planned to bring the weapons into the US to be used. 007 explained, "There is a ██████████ in another Arab country that will purchase several high-end vehicles, which will then be used as a means of transporting the weapons.

"The ████████ will be taken off, and then explosives will be placed into airtight bags, formed to fit into the ██████. Then the vehicles will be shipped into a port in North America where they will be driven to a predetermined location and disassembled. The explosives will then be re-formed to fit their intended purpose."

I couldn't help but think, *This is a rather clever way of moving explosives into the US by taking advantage of the weaknesses in our border and port security.*

007 then asked for a piece of paper and said he had to draw something to prove that what he was about to say next was true—that we would only believe

him if he drew us a schematic. He handed the paper back to me and my analyst after twenty minutes of drawing and writing engineering and physics symbols that I recognized from previous physics classes in college. Then he said, "This is the trigger mechanism that will be used in two of the VBIEDs. Do you understand what kind of trigger this is?"

I responded, "I don't, though I recognize some of the scientific symbols from college and know they're not good." I was afraid that he was about to tell me something that I wasn't going to want to hear.

"This is the trigger design for two radioactive dirty bombs that are going to be used. The first one is going to target █████ ████████ on the East Coast and the other is also going to target ████ ██████████████ ██████████ East Coast. Then suicide bombers will hit multiple random targets: police stations, a shopping mall, a movie theater, a bus and subway. The goal of the suicide bombers is to kill or maim as many people as possible and to cause Americans to fear doing normal daily activities," he said.

As he responded to all of these questions, I could see his hand shake again, which made me nervous. I wasn't sure what to make of this tic—normally, I might think the detainee was lying to me, but I also knew the gravity of information he was providing. Frankly, I was nervous just writing the report.

In my head, I was asking myself all kinds of questions like, *Is what this guy is telling me plausible? Is it believable?* I also wanted to know, *What is this man's real motivation for talking?* Further, I was worried that this information would be difficult to validate. HUMINT intelligence can be difficult to confirm sometimes because it involves taking someone, usually a very dislikable someone, at their word. It's no wonder that the process can be arduous, time-consuming, and frustrating.

My interrogation was scheduled for two hours and I had three other interrogations planned that night—I cancelled those other interrogations and continued on with 007 throughout the night and into the morning. We had been talking for nearly nine hours straight without a break. My analyst and I had taken nearly a dozen pages of notes, and it was clear 007 was exhausted and stressed from this marathon interrogation. We ended the interview with a guarantee that we would be talking again that evening.

The NCO in charge of monitoring the interrogations couldn't believe what he was hearing in our booth, so he had quickly called others to come online and watch and listen in so that there would be more people to validate what we were all being told. By the time the interrogation ended, we walked out to find individuals from our behavioral psychologist's office, two JAGs, and several other interrogators listening to the story as it was unfolding.

No one wants to believe the impossible, especially from an admitted terrorist. When the rumors about Al Qaeda flying planes into skyscrapers had surfaced, they had been ignored because the whole story seemed too crazy, too wild, and too unbelievable. But this is the type of enemy we are dealing with: insane, unpredictable, and totally dedicated to their cause.

It was an amazing and unbelievable plan. I was basically interrogating the equivalent of Mohammed Atta eighteen months prior to the September 11 attacks. The problem was the information itself. My senior leadership at the JIDC didn't believe what 007 was saying, and even worse, they were insisting that we bury this guy and forget about what we had just found.

So to add some validity to what 007 had provided us, I had him take a polygraph that evening, so we could attempt to corroborate his information. He was asked very specific questions by our three-letter agency polygrapher to determine his placement and access to the camp, and then they added some pointed questions about the plans he had told us about. To our great dismay and surprise, he passed the polygraph. This signified that he was more than likely telling us the truth, indicating that we had a real threat on our hands, no matter how bizarre it might have sounded.

After 007 passed his polygraph, we still wanted to further verify his story due to the extreme nature of his information. We wanted to test him, and so during the next interrogation, I asked him, "OK, we need you to provide us with some verifiable proof to show that you are telling the truth."

007 responded, "I can provide you with the location of a large weapon cache north of Al Khalis, not far from Baqubah."

"All right, let me get a map and you can show me where," I replied.

I procured the appropriate map, and then he proceeded to show me the specific spot, tracing the routes leading to the location with his finger and describing the contents of the weapon cache in great detail.

"There are several man-portable air-defense systems, which are the Russian version of a Stinger missile. Those are fantastic for shooting down helicopters and low-flying planes. There are also a lot of explosives being stored there; it's a way station for the materials needed to make all the IEDs and VBIEDs that are being used in the area.

"The site is a small building, well hidden under the trees and away from the main road. It's surrounded by several other buildings toward the outskirts of the city, which is an optimal location," he continued.

"When you approach the site, you need to avoid two of the roads because my old unit has spotters there, along with IEDs and VBIEDs placed at several locations along the way there. This other route here has been neglected and would be clear for you to advance."

I had him show me the specific positions of the IEDs and circled them on the map as he talked. I quickly wrote up a report that contained all this information, which was then sent to FOB Warhorse with instructions to action it immediately.

Later that day, a battalion of soldiers, several hundred of them in all, rolled out of the FOB in their Stryker vehicles and up-armored Humvees and headed to the location.

Then complete chaos broke out. The battalion commander, or someone in their group, didn't heed our warnings about approaching the enemy location from the route that 007 described and instead proceeded down one of the roads we had told them to avoid. This would be a disaster of epic proportions.

One of the Humvees was blown up by an IED, instantly killing two of the five soldiers riding inside. Then a firefight broke out and the soldiers quickly came under attack. It took them close to half an hour to secure the scene and kill or capture the men who had been shooting at them. The rest of the battalion pushed on toward the weapons cache, continuing to use the same route that we had warned them about.

The battalion got about five miles down the road when a VBIED exploded, nearly destroying one of the Stryker vehicles. Four more soldiers were killed, and everyone else in the vehicle was wounded. The same scene played out again: a firefight ensued, and then the battalion fought it out with the attackers. After securing this new scene and the evacuating the wounded, the battalion pushed on the rest of the way to the location of the weapons cache.

It took the battalion nearly four hours to get to their destination, when it should have taken them no more than thirty minutes. Upon arriving at the location, what they found was an empty building with no weapons.

Needless to say, the battalion commander was furious. He reported back to our unit that he had lost six soldiers and that nearly twenty more had been injured, all for what he considered to be a wild goose chase that we had sent him on. It shouldn't be a surprise that the boiling anger he spewed on my command rolled downhill.

My analyst and I asked what route they had taken and confirmed that it was the route we had told them to avoid. We showed them in the report that we had warned them of the danger and requested that they approach via a different route.

I don't know who was responsible for making sure they used the correct route, but we had given them the right intelligence, and they had failed to use it.

Jeremy and I were devastated to know that six US soldiers had died on the mission and more than twenty others had been injured. Even worse, we still had no weapon cache to show for it. It was hard for us to say if 007 had given us the correct information or not about the location of the weapons. Chances were, the stash was quickly moved while the battalion was trying to push through the battles to the destination. The two ambushes had slowed them down significantly and they had lost the element of surprise. What did prove to be correct was the exact locations of where the IEDs and VBIEDs were located. There was little solace in proving that point, but it did validate 007's truthfulness in our eyes, even if it resulted in the death of several Americans.

Despite the ambush, this case still posed some nearly insurmountable problems. One of the more significant snags I ran into was that during these interrogations, we were also collecting intelligence on US citizens, which was slightly outside of my charter. We were allowed to collect intelligence on US persons, but only if it was within the scope of our mission, and only if we informed the FBI and obtained their blessing. My direct commander had ordered me not to inform the FBI of my discovery until we had validated 007's identity and information to some extent. However, this presented a very real moral and legal problem. Because I had collected information regarding US persons and, more importantly, a direct threat to the US and its political leaders, it had to be reported to the FBI immediately.

I understand why our leadership at the JIDC wanted us to verify the information as much as possible—we were, after all, sitting on an incredible hot potato. But by sitting on this information, we were going to be breaking the law as well as violating numerous military regulations. Essentially, I was being asked to commit a crime. I had serious problems with this, and obviously I was not at all pleased with my superiors.

Fortunately for me, Red worked in a section that oversaw outside agency interrogations. He had personal contact with several FBI agents on a daily basis and informed one of them that they needed to request to speak to me and ask me directly what I had found. Their excuse for requesting to see me was under the guise that they had received a tip that I had found something or was withholding information from them. This was a ruse we as interrogators sometimes used with our detainees, and in this case, it worked. It allowed me to divulge much-needed information to the FBI without openly breaking a direct order from my superiors to temporarily withhold the information from the FBI.

Once I was asked directly by the FBI about the information, I was able to provide them with what I knew. They demanded that I conduct an immediate interrogation of 007 with them present so they could hear it for themselves and determine how and what to report back to their own headquarters. At this point, my leadership found out that the FBI knew about the information but was powerless in stopping the FBI from conducting the interrogation. Red was asked to insert a bug in the holding cell with 007, which he did. The FBI wasn't allowed to place bugs, but we could. This was done with the proviso that *all* information would be shared immediately after the report was filed if any info was discovered.

007 repeated the same information that he had told me to the FBI investigators. They spent six hours with him, asking copious questions and writing wildly. I can distinctly remember when the lead FBI agent said to my detainee, "I think you're making this up. There's no way Al Qaeda could carry this type of attack out."

007 took a long drag on his cigarette and leaned forward toward the FBI agent. Calmly, he responded, "When—not if, but *when* this attack happens, you remember what I told you, and remember you were the one who didn't believe it and could have stopped it."

I thought that was a pretty powerful thing to say to this FBI agent, and it looked as if it hit home. As expected, the FBI investigators were extremely alarmed and quickly wrote a FLASH report informing their director and the appropriate agencies of what they had just heard. When a FLASH report is sent, it goes straight to the top of the list to be analyzed, and in this case, it was sent immediately to the Director of the FBI, Secretary of Defense, Director of the CIA, Homeland Security, and the Vice President because it involved a very specific target and type of attack.

It didn't take long before our senior leadership was being asked to explain why they had sat on this information for ten days and failed to inform the proper agencies back home of this possible threat. As a matter of fact, it only took three hours before the Director of the FBI personally called our task force commander and inquired as to why the FBI was finding out about this information ten days after it had first been revealed. The FBI also requested the videos of the previous interrogations of 007, particularly the interrogation in which we had first learned of this plot.

Coincidentally or not, our management had somehow lost the videos. Later they said that they had been deleted from the hard drive. This was rather frustrating as we keep a copy of all interrogations on a hard drive for thirty days. One can only wonder why this interrogation video was destroyed after only ten days—and how all eight subsequent interrogation videos had been lost as well. The smell of conspiracy was in the air.

This inquisition of sorts proceeded down the rest of the chain until it ended with my direct management. They were quickly scorned, which in turn led them to speedily let me know how I had disobeyed them and made them look bad. My response was simple: "I wasn't going to lie to a federal agent, nor was I going to break the law."

I was in the right in bringing this information to the FBI and I firmly stood by my decision, despite the grief I received. Had our management allowed us to bring this information to the FBI from the beginning, there never would have been an issue. Even if the information had proved to be false or unverifiable, we still would have been OK. Our job was only to collect the information and process it so that others could analyze it for validity and try to piece together what it all meant. Though our information might not have seemed real or plausible, when combined with four or five other pieces of information from different sources, there would have been a much clearer picture of what was really going on.

Throughout this time, I dwelled on a few verses in the Bible. "Therefore, we do not lose heart. Though outwardly we are wasting away, yet inwardly we are being renewed day by day. For our light and momentary troubles are achieving for us an eternal glory that far outweighs them all. So we fix our eyes not on what is seen, but on what is unseen. For what is seen is temporary, but what is unseen is eternal" (New King James Version, 2 Cor. 4:16-19).

These verses helped me to realize that though my decision may have been unpopular, it was the right choice to make.

I later received an honorary patch and letter from the FBI for the work I had done with them on this case. I was also asked to write a formal brief of the case that was to be presented to the commanding G-2 for the Army, a three-star general who was the senior Army intelligence commander.

This was one of the largest and most complex cases I would work at the JIDC, and it was an extremely challenging case. Once the cat was out of the bag and the information we had collected was disseminated to the rest of the intelligence community, I received a lot of requests for further information. To date, I do not fully know beyond the shadow of a doubt if what he told me was one hundred percent accurate, but I do know that if even ten percent of what he said was true, we would have a serious problem.

Imagine a terrorist attack involving suicide bombers walking into several crowded malls during the holiday season and blowing themselves up. At the same time, several other suicide bombers walk into local police departments in multiple cities and begin blowing themselves up. Now couple those attacks with several 500-pound car bombs with nuclear material in the downtowns of several major cities—all of this happening at the same time on the same day. This would create mass panic and confusion, not to mention an immense number of casualties. I'm not saying that this is the type of attack my prisoner said was going to happen, but imagine if it were and you had the chance to stop it…but nobody would believe you.

Chapter 10
Banishment to the North

After six weeks of working very closely with the FBI, the Secret Service, and the CIA on the 007 case, I ran into a lull in the case and my management thought this would be a great time to banish me to northern Iraq for a short while. My sense was that my leadership felt that I had embarrassed them with the 007 case, so they wanted to put a bit of distance between me and them. Either way, my leadership had decided they wanted to get rid of me for a little bit, and since my area of expertise was everything north of Baghdad, I think they figured Mosul would be a good place to hide me for a while. Frankly, I needed a break from the JIDC and the politics that went along with working there, so going to Mosul was the best thing that could have happened to me.

I was directed to report to Forward Operating Base Diamondback, which is located at the Mosul Airport. In order to fly there, I first had to fly to Ali al Salem airbase in Kuwait. I spent my Easter Sunday shuttling from one base to another before finally arriving in Mosul; this was yet one more important holiday that I spent on the clock.

My entrance to Mosul was a rather comical one. Our C-130 flew in at around 0100 hours, and in the pitch black, our aircraft landed and came to a screeching halt at the end of the runway. No sooner had I jumped out the back of the aircraft than it took off again. I stood there in the dark for a minute wondering, *Now what?*

A few minutes later, a soldier walked out toward me, verified my name, and then said the nicest words that could have hit my ears: "I'm here to pick you up."
****

Shortly after my arrival and subsequent pickup, I received a fine welcome from the good people of Mosul in the form of a mortar attack. From my vantage point, I could see several mortars hit targets around the base while my driver and I ducked for cover. Then, almost as quickly as it started, it was over. Fortunately, no rounds landed in my immediate vicinity. Later in the week, we wouldn't be so lucky.

The FOB had a good commanding view of the city of Mosul, which is the gateway from northern Iraq to the rest of the country. I immediately loved the area—there were trees, green grass, and a semblance of home to it. I was told that I wouldn't need to constantly wear my body armor in Mosul, and after five months of lugging around an extra seventy pounds of weight in inhumanly hot temperatures, I was more than happy to leave it behind. In addition, the city is a rich tapestry of history and culture. Unfortunately, it was also a hotbed of terrorist activity.

The division holding facility there was run by elements of the 1st Cavalry Division out of Fort Bliss, Texas. They were a good group of guys, but their interrogation unit seriously lacked experienced interrogators. They had four civilian contract interrogators who were good interrogators. Each of them had experience and knew what they were doing—but again, there were only four of them. The other eight interrogators they had with them were all under twenty-four years old and lacked the necessary life experience and big-picture thinking required to be an effective interrogator.

I settled into my new position in Mosul and immediately dove into my cases, just as intensely as I had when I was in Baghdad. The typical number of cases they received in Mosul paled in comparison to the number of cases that I worked in Baghdad. This meant I brought an immense amount of experience and expertise to this group, which immediately had an impact. I made it a point to mentor the younger soldiers and share as much information as I could with them on how to run a more effective interrogation. I had just reached my third day in Mosul when I was already given the opportunity to interrogate a unique prisoner with excellent placement and access to valuable information. He had been an Iraqi Brigade S-2, a brigade intelligence officer, so if there was anyone with his finger on the Iraqi intelligence pulse, it should have been this guy. CF had detained this Iraqi colonel because there was suspicion that he might be providing intelligence to terrorists.

After several days of interrogations, it became clear that he was not passing information to the terrorists but rather had gotten caught trying to obtain information from them. As an intelligence officer, he was attempting to gain access to the terrorist organizations by renewing contact with an old friend from before the war who was now working with the terrorists. The colonel was hoping to work out a give-and-take agreement with this friend. His plan might have worked, had he not been conducting his intelligence operations using a cell phone, which was subsequently intercepted by Coalition Forces.

Though he was upset about being detained, the colonel agreed to talk and started providing a vast amount of information. He began, "A mosque near the old city of Mosul is being used as a primary means of funneling money into northern Iraq from Saudi Arabia."

I leaned in, and he continued, "The money is being used to provide financial support to the Al Qaeda groups operating in northern Iraq. This particular mosque is also being used as a recruitment center for Al Qaeda as well as a safe house for foreign fighters traveling into Iraq from other countries in the Middle East. I am not able to act on this information, so hopefully you can."

He continued to talk freely, spilling the beans on a plethora of information regarding Al Qaeda financing and its leadership structure in Mosul. Since I currently had his undying attention as a guest of my detainment facility, I thought I would ask my Iraqi colonel about the corruption that was so rampant in Iraq. Anyone who read or watched the news at all knew there was a lot of dishonesty and mismanagement going on. Even though I had spent a vast amount of each day conducting interrogations and writing reports, I had still managed to spend some time reading news sources like *The Economist* magazine and looking through different news outlets on the Internet. Since I wasn't entirely living in the pit of my interrogation booth, I had good conversational topics to discuss with my more intellectually inclined prisoners.

I opened the dialogue on this topic by asking him about supplies and equipment shortages. Before he could respond, I poured him a cup of hot chai and brought out some fresh dates.

He happily took the snack and then explained, "The Americans give my brigade a certain number of fuel trucks worth of fuel each month. This fuel is to be used for our vehicles and for conducting patrols in the city. However, the brigade commander had two of his sergeants take one of the fuel trucks to a city near Mosul and sell the fuel on the open market."

He took a sip of tea, ate a couple of dates, and then continued, "The fuel was sold for about six thousand US dollars a month, which was distributed equally to the people involved. This scheme caused the brigade to run short on fuel, and in the end, it couldn't carry out all of its operations in the city."

To further add to this corruption, the colonel told me about the actual troop numbers in the brigade and battalions. He explained, "About ten percent of each of the three battalions in my brigade will not show up for work. They paid their battalion and brigade commanders a cut of their monthly paycheck, and in exchange, they do not have to come to work." So here the Iraqi Army was, reporting to the US a particular number of operational combat troops, but in actuality, that number was much lower.

As if this were not enough, he continued, "The commanding general in Mosul has some 300 employees to do reconstruction work in and around Mosul, whose wages are being paid to him by the US government. Only, the projects are fictitious, and so are the workers. It's all a plot to fatten this general's pocket at the expense of the US government."

I was flabbergasted at the amount and depth of corruption within the Iraqi Army and wondered if I even wanted to dig further. I determined at this point that this colonel was most likely involved in this fraud, and it looked more and more likely that he probably had some involvement with Al Qaeda as well. No one could know this much detail and not be mixed up with them at some level.

I wanted to believe this man when he said he was just trying to gather intelligence about Al Qaeda and provide it to the Coalition Forces—and I did, at first. But it did seem odd that he knew so much about the organization: names, locations, and methods of financing. The more I heard from him, the harder it was to think that he could not be involved with the terrorists to some extent.

Truthfully, it didn't make a difference if he was just another corrupt Iraqi Army officer or not; he had information of value, and he was cooperative. I managed to produce twelve IIRs over a seven-day period—this accounted for about sixty percent of the unit's intelligence collection that month.

Much to my amazement and surprise, the cavalry unit operating in Mosul acted on the information within days of my reports being published and captured a top-ten-ranking Al Qaeda leader operating in northern Iraq. We also managed to capture over two dozen other prisoners and seriously disrupted their operations in northern Iraq. For once, I had the sweet taste of victory without some accompanying struggle.

****

A few days later, while I was walking back to the office after dinner, my eyes wandered, and I scanned the sky. I thought I had heard something…maybe someone yelling or a car crash. Suddenly—*boom*! An enormous explosion ripped through the air, and I could feel the ground beneath me tremble. I was just outside the building I worked in, so I ran inside to find out if they knew anything. Then I heard the sound of numerous machine guns going off and several smaller secondary explosions.

The chief warrant officer in charge of us told us, "Just sit tight in the building while I try to find out what's going on."

I was frantically thinking to myself, *Do I have a battle position I'm supposed to man? Should I put my body armor on and grab my rifle?*

The chief returned a few minutes later and said the main gate had just been hit with a VBIED. He explained, "The gate is under attack, but the troops there have it under control. So just stay put for now."

So, like any good soldier would do, we wandered up to the roof so we could try to get a better look at what was transpiring. After all, the fighting was happening no more than 2,000 yards away from us.

Off in the distance, I could see a plume of black smoke where the VBIED had gone off, and several guard towers were firing tracer rounds into a couple of buildings and the surrounding area. Then I heard helicopter blades swishing through the air and saw a pair of gunships swoop in to engage the insurgents, firing a few rockets into a building.

The structure that the American soldiers had been shooting at completely blew up. One of the helicopters turned hard as it climbed back into the sky, reaching for altitude, and then made a tight circle as it came in for another run. As it turned back toward the fighting on the ground, its 30mm machine gun strafed at its targets.

I looked up behind me and saw a new pair of Apache attack helicopters moving in to join the fray. They launched several rockets into some buildings and opened fire with their own machine guns. Slowly, the shooting dissipated as the sunset signaled the day's end. As the darkness approached and became final, the fighting ended altogether, and a semblance of calm emerged.

We found out later that night that the main entry control point to the base, which was manned by the Iraqi police, had been hit with a 5,000-pound VBIED that had blown the entire entrance apart. Some fifteen Iraqi police officers had been killed and dozens more had been injured. No Americans had been killed in the blast, although several had been injured from the explosion and the ensuing gun battle.

The true target of the attack was not so much the Americans as it was the Iraqis. The Al Qaeda cells in the city had been changing their tactics, and they were targeting the local police more and more. Their goal was to cause enough fear that people would not want to work with the government of Iraq or the Americans. Personally, I think it only drove the Iraqi people toward cooperation with the Americans, rather than away from it.

Although the level of violence in Mosul was nothing like it was in Baghdad, we still received several mortar attacks in addition to our most recent attack on the main entry control point. The morning after the conflict, I was interrogating a detainee who had been caught early in the morning shooting at an American convoy as it was patrolling through the same neighborhood where all the fighting had taken place. We sat in our small interrogation room, and as I was asking him which organization he was working for, the base suddenly received three mortar rounds, all of which landed rather close to my interrogation booth. The concussion from the blast was enough that the prisoner bounced out of his chair and onto the floor. My pen and paper sprung off the table as well.

I knew at that point I had two choices: I could freak out and let this piece of trash see me act anything other than godlike, or I could pretend the attack had not happened and continue on. I chose to carry on and screamed at the top of my lungs, "*Stop falling out of your chair!* This kind of act *will not* get you out of trouble or keep you from answering my questions!"

He was obviously rather shaken up by the event, and he even peed in his pants. However, he also began to provide me with the information I was looking for.

At the exact moment in time when those mortars hit near us, I realized that I could use his fear of the situation to get this guy to crack by applying a very harsh and mean approach. At just about any other time, that approach would most likely have not worked on him since he was a pretty staunch AQI supporter. I saw an opportunity to go after him in a moment of weakness and took it. After that experience, I realized that sometimes what works in one set of circumstances is unique to the events surrounding it.

****

While I was in Mosul, I had the opportunity to do something truly exciting. I was able to leave the box of my interrogation booth and do some sightseeing. I toured a site that most people will never even dream of being able to see—the Dair Mar Elia monastery, a Christian monastery that dates back to 400 AD. It is a beautiful ancient site with high walls to keep out intruders. There are numerous small structures inside it and a cathedral built into one of the walls, which was spectacular to see. The outer walls were surrounded by rolling green hills and meadows covered in wildflowers. It was peaceful being there; my mind could rest and just soak up the view and the fresh air. I believe that I read on the news that this place has now been desecrated by ISIS—it is truly a shame to think that after surviving for hundreds of years, this monastery is no longer a heritage site for future generations.

Right next to the monastery was a boneyard of old nonoperational Iraqi Army vehicles and tanks from the Soviet era. There were seven of us guys touring the monastery, so naturally, after our tour, we made our way over to the boneyard and explored, wandering through the various vehicles. It was awe-inspiring to be able to crawl through a T-72 tank, other armored personnel carriers, and antiaircraft vehicles. We took lots of pictures for the folks at home of all of us pretending to operate the machinery or firing retired missile launchers.

Unfortunately, shortly after exploring the boneyard, it was time for us to head back to our base and get some lunch before going back to work.
****

Now having had several years to reflect on my time in Mosul, I do feel angry and a bit betrayed by our government and particularly by the policies of Hillary Clinton and President Obama. We lost a lot of good men and women securing Mosul and northern Iraq, and now it's controlled by the Islamic State in the Levant, or ISIS. How could all the hard work and sacrifice we made be so easily and thoughtlessly thrown away by our leaders? As Secretary of State, Hillary Clinton should have had the forethought and vision to know what would happen in Iraq if we pulled all our forces out. She was given numerous warnings and counsel by key intelligence and military leaders about the dangers of withdrawing, yet she guided the President toward this policy of leaving Iraq.

President Obama and Hillary Clinton could have used economic and military aid to persuade the Iraqi government to sign a Status of Forces Agreement and maintain an enduring presence to continue to train and mentor the Iraqi Army. Had they done this, we would not have seen nearly one-third of Iraq fall to ISIL and the rest of the country become an Iranian proxy. Now America finds itself in the situation of having to send US forces back into Iraq to help the Iraqis retake their country from terrorists. There is no way we can view this as a diplomatic victory or a win of any kind, yet that is what Secretary Clinton continued to tout. It's hard for me to look at all the hard work that I and my fellow men and women in arms put into Iraq and not feel that it was squandered by poor decisions at the top.
****

All in all, I enjoyed my time in Mosul and would have chosen to stay there, but my leadership element back in Baghdad saw the direct impact of my absence. I was now accounting for forty percent of the intelligence production being written by my section, and the lowered report production in my section was messing with their stats. In the three weeks I was gone, my northern Iraq team back near Baghdad, which consisted of eight interrogators, had produced a paltry twenty intelligence reports. In contrast, I had produced an additional twelve reports alone while I was in Mosul. Given this disruption in group stats, I was recalled back to Baghdad to restart my old cases again and continue to do what I did best: get information.

Chapter 11
Return from Exile

I dreaded returning to Baghdad, but that was where I was needed the most, so that was where I went. Once again, I was back in the thick of things, and I resumed some of my cases that had been active prior to me going to Mosul.

During my second week back in Baghdad, I received a new high-value detainee, Abu Saif. He had been a top-twenty-five high-value individual, or HVI, in the northern Baghdad belt, leading a VBIED cell.

I had to marvel at how this particular HVI was captured. Our targeting groups had been monitoring Abu Saif through the use of his ███ ██████ electronic device. Coalition Forces had identified his exact location and moved in with a Delta Force team to capture him while he was driving. A little bird helicopter was providing overwatch and videoing the takedown while a Blackhawk helicopter went in for the kill.

A Special Forces member leaned out of the side of the helicopter with his rifle and fired several rounds into the hood of Abu Saif's vehicle. Once the SUV stopped, three Special Forces guys jumped out of the helicopter on ropes, ran over, and pulled him out of the driver's-side window. One of the SF soldiers zip-tied his hands, put a hood over his head and threw him over his back, and ran to the Blackhawk, which had now landed in the center of the street. It was the most spectacular snatch-and-grab I'd ever seen recorded. I only wish I could've burned a copy of it to take home with me.

Unfortunately, I was unable to get Abu Saif's separation package approved in a timely manner due to the legal requirements placed on us, and he was placed into the general population for three days before his paperwork was finished moving through the chain of command. Since we couldn't put him or any detainee in a holding cell by themselves without approval, during that three-day period, he was coached by fellow detainees and was able to cement his cover story together. It proved to be a frustrating week of interrogations and ultimately led me to obtaining no information of intelligence value despite the numerous approaches and techniques I tried. For me, this was extremely frustrating as I typically had a very high success rate. For all the glory of his capture, we had to chalk up one more missed opportunity because of the 2005 Detainee Treatment Act, which has seriously hampered our ability to act quickly and with some degree of latitude in interrogating prisoners. Thanks, John McCain.

****

Shortly after that debacle, I decided to go ahead and spend some time with one of my other cases with whom I hadn't talked in a while. Although most of my cases had been handed over to someone else when I had gone to Mosul, I still had a couple of my long-term detainees, my pet projects. I started talking with 007 again and figured I'd try to see what other areas of interest I could exploit.

Like a moth is attracted to the light, I was drawn to this case. He was interesting, yet very disturbing…he had committed some terribly violent acts of terrorism. Nonetheless, he was completely broken as a prisoner and willing to talk. This made him unusual—most prisoners with his level of information and previous intelligence training tend to resist interrogation and reveal very little in the way of valuable intelligence. Though there were times when I had my doubts about his cooperation and the level of information he was providing, he truly had converted to being not just a willing source, but to helping secure his country. I had spent the better part of four months talking with him at this point, and it was almost as if he had become a victim of Stockholm Syndrome, relating to his captors and siding with us.

We started to discuss his motives for joining Al Qaeda, which stemmed from a myriad of reasons but mainly came down to money. He was being paid two thousand US dollars a month as a commander of about two hundred fighters. He was also responsible for recruiting additional fighters into his group and coordinating attacks against Coalition Forces. His particular group was broken down into three elements, with several small groups for more specialized operations.

Being that 007 was a former military officer and had served in the Iraqi Special Forces, he broke his organization down into three companies, forming a regiment. One company was in charge of carrying out IED, VBIED, and various other forms of attacks against Coalition Forces and Iraqi Army units. This group was responsible for a good number of the roadside bomb deaths that were continually being reported in the American media. The second company was to blame for the acquisition of various weapons and explosives and protecting the storehouses. This group also carried out mortar and rocket attacks against Forward Operating Base Warhorse and the local Iraqi Army base near the Baqubah airport. I particularly disliked this group because I remembered all the times I was trying to sleep or eat at the chow hall when a mortar attack suddenly ensued. Even if the mortars weren't always accurate, they left the troops with a constant feeling of uneasiness.

The third group was responsible for kidnappings and various other intelligence operations. The abductions were an important method of financing the regiment, as the large ransoms that were demanded supported the other terrorist activities. If the family paid the money, then they got their family member back—if they didn't, the family member was killed. This tactic usually provided the AQI group with around twenty to forty thousand dollars a month in additional revenue. Most of the people targeted for kidnapping tended to be Iraqis who were working for the government or the Army. This was usually done not just for the money but also to deter anyone from wanting to work with the Americans or the government of Iraq.

007 also told me how he had worked aggressively to eliminate some of his rival organizations. His enemies were many, including the Jaysh al Mahdi, which is a Shi'a insurgent organization primarily under the leadership of Muqtada al Sadar; the Badr Corps, a Shi'a political organization that also has a strong military arm as well, funded and supported by the Iranian government and routinely receiving its support and training by the Iranian intelligence apparatus; and the 1920th Revolutionary Brigade, an insurgent organization. The Badr Corps is particularly troublesome because it represents a direct intervention by the Iranian government in an attempt to destabilize the government of Iraq, as well as a way for the Iranians to kill Americans without directly challenging us. All of these groups operate in virtually every major city in Iraq and have some degree of influence in most of the smaller villages throughout Iraq.

One day while chatting with 007, he disclosed some particularly valuable information regarding his regiment's intelligence apparatus. After he took a long puff on the cigarette I had allowed him to have, he smiled his sinister smile and said, "You know, it's a wonder that you all haven't found the spies in your camp yet."

"What do you mean?" I countered.

"My regiment has placed several informants in the Iraqi Army, the National Guard, and as interpreters working on the American bases."

Seeing that the average American doesn't speak or understand Arabic, the Army routinely used local nationals as interpreters. We needed to be able to trust these people. I knew that the majority of interpreters were loyal and good people, but it was scary to think what a few bad apples among them could achieve.

Red had run into one of these dubious interpreters while questioning a man. He asked the man how he felt about the Americans being in his country and capturing Saddam Hussein.

The man said, "I'm glad you came, but it's time to go."

Now, this was an entirely fair and coherent answer, and one that he had heard before. However, when Red asked the interpreter what the man had said, he responded, "He no like Americans. He said he wants you to get the hell out of his country."

This was a classic case of Shi'a/Sunni hatred. We were always wary for this kind of bias.

I thought I would stroke 007's ego a little bit. "Tell me more about the interpreters. I want to know how your system works. How do you manage to fool us with them?"

007 almost chuckled and with delight told me, "They work as double agents. They provide you with good information on the local area, and they are helpful enough not to arouse suspicion. However, at the same time, they are also collecting information for my regiment."

He paused, took another puff on his cigarette, and continued, "These double agents help us avoid capture, and they identify patrol and convoy routes for the regiment to attack. All the while, you never suspect a thing."

I shuddered to think just how much damage a few traitors could really do to the Coalition Forces. The thought didn't sit well with me as I went to sleep that night.

It was ironically during the same time period that I was interrogating 007 about this subject that I was handed an interpreter who had been detained on suspicion of providing information to Al Qaeda, although this interpreter had no relationship with 007's group. I must admit, I enjoyed interrogating this particular interpreter. He spoke excellent English and we conducted our entire interrogation in English, which of course was much easier for me than constantly having everything translated to and from Arabic.

I asked him, "Abbas, is there any truth to what is being said about you?"

At first, he said, "No, it is all false. Lies that people made up against me because they don't like me."

I said, "I would like to believe you. I'm going to conduct a polygraph on you to verify that what you're saying is correct." I explained, "The results of the polygraph will be used in an Iraqi court—"

Once I said that, Abbas immediately asked me, "Can I start over?"

I calmly replied, "Because I'm an understanding man, I will agree to allow you a second chance."

At that point, I also gave him a cup of tea. As he sipped it, he told me about his connection with the terrorists. Abbas began, "I have been working as an interpreter with the Americans for the past two years. About a year ago, an Al Qaeda member approached me and told me that if I did not provide him with information on the Americans and work with him, they would kidnap my family and kill them. I did not have a choice. I *had* to work for them or they would kill my family."

A tear trickled down his cheek. In a muffled voice, he muttered, "I don't want to be a traitor, but I didn't know what to do."

Seeing the mental state that Abbas was now in, I chose to take on a more compassionate, sympathetic role with him. I told him, "If you had said this from the beginning, we could have helped your family."

He nodded and replied, "I was afraid."

Through numerous interrogations of Abbas, I was able to catch a glimpse of the level of Al Qaeda infiltration. He admitted to working for Al Qaeda and using the Americans to help eliminate some of the other organizations operating in Baqubah and the surrounding areas. Abbas provided the Americans with information from another Al Qaeda–planted source on the location of key JAM members or weapon caches. The Americans naturally would act on this information, detain the JAM members in question, and thus remove a threat to the local AQI group.

However, the information about JAM was not without a price. Since AQI could find out from their interpreter moles exactly where the Americans would be and when they would be coming, they would set up IEDs and ambush routes for the soldiers once they had detained the JAM members. It was a two-for-one deal for AQI; their enemy JAM was removed as a threat, and they could carry out an attack on American forces.

After many conversations with Abbas, we identified a total of nine other interpreters who had been working with Al Qaeda and some who had been working for Jaysh al Mahdi. As disturbing as this discovery was, there was little we could do about it. We detained the crooked interpreters, and the Iraqi government charged them with treason, but there wasn't very much that we could do to determine the legitimacy of the rest of the interpreters we frequently used.

All of the interpreters at the JIDC where I worked were top-notch interpreters. They were all American citizens and had either secret or top-secret security clearances. However, at the tactical level out in the field, this was not the case. The interpreters used on field missions tended to be local nationals who had families living among the community. Unfortunately, not living in the protected areas of the bases made the interpreters and their families extremely susceptible to being coerced by local Al Qaeda groups. It looked like this was just one more thing we were going to have to live with and keep a close eye on.
****

As tight as the security was at the JIDC, we also had our own problems with protecting information. A friend of mine had gotten a new detainee from the Al Anbar province who had been captured with a 200GB computer hard drive that contained a truckload of information about Al Qaeda operations: names, phone numbers, and other important pieces of information. Unfortunately, the hard drive also contained a vast amount of information that was alarming and very surprising.

It had over 20,000 SECRET classified intelligence files of existing detainees, which included the document exploitation we had done, cellular phone exploitation, media exploitation, link diagrams of what we knew about the Al Qaeda groups across Iraq and the Middle East, maps, and all the interrogator notes and intelligence information reports that had been written up to the point it had been downloaded. It was a complete and absolute operational security nightmare that had just been uncovered.

The proper authorities were "notified," but from my perspective, nothing came of it. My friend quickly lost the case as it was taken over by "management," and nothing was ever said about it. People were ordered not to talk about it and just be quiet. What was unbelievable to me was that we now knew we had a traitor in our midst who was working directly with Al Qaeda, yet our management was telling us to not worry about it and be quiet—but I digress.

Chapter 12
Coercion and Manipulation

One day, I was handed five new cases to go along with the twelve I was already trying to juggle. I simply didn't have enough time in the day or enough days in the week to effectively handle five new cases. I elected to try something different with my new detainees. I wrote out my interrogation plans and planned on doing all five interrogations on the same evening. I would conduct them over a four-hour period of time from 0130 to 0530, and yes, that's in the middle of the night. It made for a long couple of days.

Fortunately, in my private life, I had a major victory right about then. I was back down to one roommate. Oh, what a difference only having one other person to wake me up made. It made all the craziness at work so much more tolerable, and I suddenly found myself thinking much more clearly.

The next day, my interpreter and I went out to our interrogation booth early and set up the room with a table dividing the room in half and two chairs behind the table, one for myself and one for my interpreter. We turned up the heat and made it extremely warm and rather uncomfortable. To ensure we didn't violate any regulations, we made sure there were several bottles of water next to the chair that the detainee would sit in so that he would have plenty to drink, if he chose to drink. I brought in several of my current case files, which were extremely large, and placed them on the table for effect. On the walls, we hung several maps of each of the locations these five detainees lived in and the places that they were captured at.

Once I had staged the booth, I pulled the men in one at a time. I had the first prisoner stand in front of my table and answer some basic questions. I asked him, "Do you enjoy being detained, or would you like to go home?"

He obviously replied, "I want to go home."

I let him know, "I will work to get you released, but only if you answer some questions."

So he stated, "I will do my best."

Then I said, "Go ahead and sit down. Drink some water if you would like."

After he took a seat, I proceeded to ask him, "Who have you heard of in your village or city that is working with the terrorists?"

The man gave me the staple response, "*Wa Allah Ma'arf*"—"I swear to God, I don't know."

Without letting this get under my skin, I told him, "We have been monitoring you for some time." Then I held up one of my thick folders to illustrate the amount of information I had on him.

He continued to deny any involvement or information regarding terrorists in his area, so I informed him, "You will be sent to Camp Bucca for long-term confinement while you await trial."

He just hung his head down and said, "I have no information to provide. Please don't send me to Camp Bucca."

It was clear that this man wasn't going to give up any information of intelligence value, so I dismissed him and had him sent to Camp Bucca, which was a massive detainment camp down in southern Iraq near Basrah. It housed some twenty thousand detainees, and typically once people were sent there, they simply fell into a broken system that tended to have them detained for years rather than staying at Camp Cropper, where at least they stood a chance of getting released within six months.

I pulled in my next detainee, Omar, and repeated the process that I had started with the first man all over again. I asked him, "Who is working with the terrorists in your village?"

At this point, Omar was extremely tired and exhausted and admitted, "There are six people in my village working with the terrorists."

Surprised that he gave me an honest answer, I asked him, "What organization do they belong to?"

He informed me, "They are part of Al Qaeda."

I inquired, "What are their names?"

Amazingly, he told me all six names. Then I let Omar know, "I will keep you here with me at Camp Cropper. Do not talk to the other prisoners about what we discussed. If you are willing to continue to work with me, I will work to help get you released sooner."

He immediately replied, "Yes, I agree to your terms."

With that, I told him, "I will speak with you in a couple of days. You are dismissed."

Unfortunately, the other three detainees I interrogated that day weren't willing to cut a deal with me, so I had them sent to Camp Bucca and focused my attentions on the one that was willing to cooperate.

A couple of days later, I called Omar back in and we began to talk about his village. He was from northwestern Iraq, from a village near the Syrian border. His town was not a particularly large community, but it sat along the Euphrates River and was next to a key bridge that crossed it.

Omar told me about the trouble these six people had been causing in his village. "These AQI members threaten people in order to get them to work for the terrorists. If a person doesn't work for AQI and do as they say, the AQI members will kill their family."

Omar wrung his hands together nervously and then continued, "They approached me one day and said, 'If you do not place this IED near the entrance of the road, we will kill your father.' If I wanted my family to live, I did not have a choice, so I did as I was told. This went on for several months until I was captured for placing an IED."

Omar begged me, "If I tell you the location of the terrorist members, will you go and arrest them?"

I assured him, "If you tell me where these men are, we will send the Marines after them."

Omar smiled, relaxed a little bit, and proceeded to give me more detail about the AQI members, their locations, and what they did in the organization. He also told me who was building the IEDs and how they were obtaining their equipment to build them. As Omar continued, he explained, "The AQI members are getting their weapons and explosives from Syria."

I was curious. "How are they getting them into Iraq? Is it via standard roads or some hidden back road?"

Omar responded, "The explosives come in from the river. A fishing boat floats down the river from Syria with the explosives and weapons."

Still curious, I inquired, "How do they manage to get the weapons past the patrol boats that are also on the river?"

Omar replied, "They wrap the explosives or weapons together and then drag them behind and underneath the boat with a rope in a barrel that they submerge. This enables them to smuggle the weapons undetected."

Omar said, "Fishing boats don't travel at a high rate of speed, so there is little in the way of drag when the boat is pulling the weapons underwater. If the boat traveled faster, then the weapons would rise toward the surface as they were being pulled, giving them away. This is why fishing boats were ideal for this type of operation."

I couldn't help but think, *This is a rather ingenious way of moving weapons across the border.*

My analyst and I wrote up a report about our findings and quickly received feedback from the Marines stationed out in this village. They detained all the people Omar had talked about and found several IEDs at one of the houses. There were also components to build numerous other IEDs at a second house. Later in

91

the month, the Marines stopped a fishing boat on the river, and sure enough, they found weapons being towed behind it.

Omar turned out to be an okay guy. I mean, sure, he placed IEDs along the side of the road to try to kill Americans, but he was coerced into doing it, and when he had the chance to rat out the people who'd forced him to do it, he did. We neutralized an entire IED cell operating in this particular region of Iraq because of his information. I think of how many people we might have saved just with this one cell eliminated, and I knew we had earned our pay for the day.

I wrote Omar a good letter of recommendation and explained how his information had led to the arrest of numerous AQI members. I placed it in his file, and that was the end of it from my side of things. I honestly have no idea if Omar was ever released or further detained. I just moved on to the next case and went after the next cell.

Looking back on this case, I can't help but wonder whether I might have found more information about the AQI members operating in the area if I had pressed Omar further. Or maybe I could have had those AQI members we caught transferred to me.

In April of 2008, six months after I came home, I learned of a death: one of my friends from church that I had grown up with had a brother serving as a Marine, and he was killed by an IED in the same area as Omar's village. Three other Marines died with him as well. I'll never know for certain, but I feel that if I had pressed further, I might have gotten a few more names out of that group of people, and perhaps we could have captured or killed the AQI members who killed my friend's brother.
****

Up to this point, one thing I had learned from my time in Iraq was how coerced and manipulated the average Iraqi was by terrorists. Ironically, I had to constantly use manipulation tactics on them as well; it was a balancing act on a tightrope to make sure that I didn't break the rules. However, it was extremely important that I never cross the fine line into coercing them.

I could plant an idea or thought in my detainee's mind and let him connect the dots, but I, as the interrogator, could not connect them for him. If I did, I would cross the line. For example, when we were back in Arizona completing our training, if my fellow trainee and I said something like, "If you do not provide me with the information, I will lock you away for the rest of your life, and you will *never* see your family again!" it would be a direct threat, and incidentally I would not have that kind of authority or power to lock him away anyway. By using an open threat and coercing my detainee to give me information, I would have just violated the 2005 Detainee Treatment Act and several regulations in the FM 2.22-3 Interrogation Field Manual, which was our interrogation bible.

Using manipulation is similar but not quite coercion. I often used this technique when I would say things like, "If you do not provide me with the information…you will *most likely* be found guilty by the Iraqi Criminal Court, and it *may* be a long time before you get to see your family again." The differences may seem small, but they are very important. The slight differences in my choice of words could mean the difference between an effective interrogation that stays within the guidelines of the law, and an interrogation that may or may not provide results and could get me sent home for violations of US law. I was determined to make it through to the end of the mission.
****

Soon after I finished talking with Omar, I was given a fifteen-year-old kid named Mi'ad to interrogate. He was from a small village just outside of Baqubah and was detained because he got caught placing an IED on the side of the road as a convoy was approaching his village. But unlike Omar, Mi'ad was not just some innocent young kid who had been forced to do something against his will. He came from a family of IED builders, and we were hot after them. The problem was we didn't know where his family had fled to.

I sat him down in the chair and grilled him. "Where has your father gone to?"

He just smirked and said, "You know where he is."

So I asked a slightly different question. "Are your father and brothers hiding with someone else?"

Again, Mi'ad just smiled and tried to play dumb. "You know where they are."

Seeing this little punk smile and smirk at me and my questions infuriated me. American soldiers were getting killed each week by the IEDs his family was placing in our area. He apparently didn't understand the gravity of his situation, and so I changed gears. I whispered to my interpreter, "I'm about to go all 'bad cop' on this kid. Play along, OK?"

Then without notice, I jumped out of my chair and lunged at the kid, bringing my face within an inch of his. I screamed directly at him at the top of my lungs, "Where are your father and brothers? I want to know *now*!" I slammed my hand on the table.

Mi'ad nearly fell out of his chair and then jumped back up into the corner of the interrogation room, trying to hide from me. "I don't know. I don't know."

Now that I had Mi'ad off guard, I continued to push him harder. I again moved closer to him until my face was within inches of him. Then I moved over to one of his ears and said quietly, "It will be OK…just tell me where your father is."

I pulled out a map of Mi'ad's village and told him to identify for me the location where his father might be hiding out with his brothers. When he didn't respond, I moved to his other ear and then screamed, "Show me *now*!" Then I slammed my hand on the table with the map on it, making a loud cracking sound as my wedding ring hit the metal table.

Mi'ad just sank to the floor and cried, muttering, "I can't tell you…you'll kill them."

I switched roles again and sat down on the floor next to Mi'ad and told him softly, "If you tell me where they are, we can arrest them at night when they're sleeping so they won't get hurt. This way we can detain them, and they won't get injured."

Mi'ad whimpered, "I want your word that you won't kill them."

I assured him, "If you tell us where they are, we will try to do everything we can to detain them and not hurt them. We just want to talk to them, not kill them."

Finally, he admitted, "OK, they are staying with a relative who lives near the edge of the village by the school."

I had Mi'ad point out the exact house and tell me a little about the home, how many people lived there, whether they had any weapons, and some other questions important to know prior to the raid.

I told him, "If you're lying to me about this location, you may be detained a lot longer. You will be seen as cooperating further with the terrorists, and that will be added to your charges."

He pleaded, "That's the correct house. I'm not lying."

With that stressful interrogation done, my analyst Jeremy and I wrote up the report about the location of these IED builders and sent it off to a local unit in the area. Two days after we provided the report to the local units, they raided the home.

Unfortunately, during my interrogation of Mi'ad, I had failed to ask a question about the home's details—I had forgotten to ask if the main doors had a secondary lock on them other than the main keyhole lock. As it turned out, the house had a lock on the floor and the ceiling, providing the door with additional reinforcement. The Army unit conducting the raid went to knock down the door with a ram, but it didn't fully open. They had to hit the door numerous times and then eventually had to shoot the hinges and the ceiling and floor locks off.

With all the noise, Mi'ad's father and brothers had woken up and grabbed their weapons and attacked the soldiers trying to breach the house. The report from the Army unit told us they ended up having a thirty-minute gun battle with the people in the house and eventually leveled the house with several rockets from a gunship. Two Americans had been injured, and the targets of the raid had been killed, a total of eight enemy dead. The Army unit sent me and Jeremy some pictures of the corpses and asked if we could have Mi'ad identify them to confirm that it was his father and brothers.

The following day, I had to bring Mi'ad back in for interrogation. I informed him, "I need you to identify some people for me. They were killed trying to fight the Americans."

He replied, "I will do my best."

Then I pulled the photos out of my folder and showed them to Mi'ad. He took them and then suddenly broke out with tears and started crying and wailing. "That's my father and brothers…you *killed* them. You said you wouldn't kill them if I told you where they were!"

All I could do at this point was tell Mi'ad that I was sorry and say, "They got killed, but they attacked the Americans. We had no choice but to kill them."

I remember Mi'ad just sitting there in his chair crying and knowing that there was nothing I could do for him. Seeing that there wasn't anything for me to do, I collected the photos, got up and walked out of the room.

I felt bad about the whole case. I had manipulated Mi'ad into giving us the information we needed and promised him we wouldn't kill his family, yet that was exactly what we did. The human side of me felt bad for this kid, but at the same time I had to remember that this same adolescent whom I was feeling bad for had tried to kill several Americans with a roadside bomb no more than a month earlier. His family had been responsible for numerous Americans being killed. Why should I feel bad for him or his family?

Given the same opportunity, his family would have killed me and my friends. Eliminating them probably saved several other families in the US from receiving the news that their loved one had been killed by a roadside bomb. Knowing all this, however, didn't make it any easier. We had just traded one life for another, eight Iraqis for an unknown number of Americans.

Chapter 13
Operation Pericles and Diyala River Valley

In the early summer of 2007, the US Army was at full strength from the troop surge of an additional 30,000 combat troops and was ready to go on the offensive. Before that, during the spring of 2007, the Al Anbar province of Iraq was having a "come to Jesus" reality check and realized that siding with and working with the terrorists wasn't panning out so well for them. What emerged was something called "The Awakening." This revival of sorts was taking place among the top tribal sheiks in the province, and they had begun to put their foot down on the terrorists operating in their territories. They were no longer taking the passive role of bystanders and created a security force of their own called the Sons of Iraq. They were of course being paid by the Americans via the Iraqi government, but they were now actively engaging themselves in cleansing their areas of Al Qaeda operatives. This was exactly what the Coalition Forces had been striving to achieve for the last couple of years, and it was now fully coming to fruition.

Because of "The Awakening," Al Qaeda shifted their forces and attacks from the Al Anbar province to the neighboring Diyala province, which of course was my primary area of concern. Around the May/June timeframe of 2007, General Petraeus ordered an additional two combat brigades to Baqubah to begin a full search and destroy operation of the area. This additional buildup of troops in and around the city of Baqubah set the stage for what became one of the hottest areas of fighting since the 2004 and 2005 battles of Fallujah. With close to 25,000 US forces and twice as many Iraqi forces, the search-and-destroy operations began in earnest.

Operation Arrowhead Ripper was the first of several major operations conducted in the Diyala province that summer. The area commander completely quarantined the city of about half a million people and called it "detained" until he had rooted out the terrorists. Though there was significant fighting as the Army cleared the city block by block, the operation had been too largely publicized prior to its initiation. The bulk of the Al Qaeda forces slipped out into the Diyala River Valley just north of the city.

The process continued on for several weeks with mixed results. There were several people detained, and there was some significant fighting as some Al Qaeda groups chose to stay and fight. But the operation didn't fully accomplish its stated goals. Once the fighting had ended and the quarantine was lifted, the Al Qaeda groups moved right back into the city.

As I was listening to the news and reading the reports of these events unfolding, I couldn't help but find the idea of rooting Al Qaeda out rather funny in a way. As wonderful as it sounded, it was rather impractical, if not impossible to do. The terrorists simply faded into the population and disappeared. In asymmetrical warfare, those rules change a bit.

To battle this problem, the US military established hundreds of small combat outposts and stationed platoons in virtually every sizable village across the major hot spots in Iraq. This allowed for continuous patrols throughout the neighborhoods and showed the communities that the Americans were not leaving. As the number of detainees being captured increased, the amount of HUMINT intelligence being collected amplified, and more missions were able to be actioned. When I started my tour, we were receiving 200 to 300 new detainees a week to interrogate. Once the surge was in full swing, that number jumped up to 600 to 800 a week. As soon as the JIDC published an IIR, the local unit in the area would be sent out to act on the information. This strategy became a real turning point in the war. The enemy was actively being hunted down and killed or captured, which was reducing the level of violence in Iraqi villages immensely.

During this struggle, I received a prisoner who was an imam in his village. He was, like most Sunnis, suspected of working for Al Qaeda, and was therefore handed to me to see what I could get from him. Imam Ali was born with a crippled leg and required arm crutches to move around. I started our session off with some hot tea and a warm, inviting smile. I liked Ali from the get-go. He had such an optimistic attitude despite his physical handicap and the hardships he now had to endure as a detainee at Camp Cropper.

I asked him, "So what happened? Why don't you explain to me the accusations being made against you?"

He replied, "I had been one of the moderate voices in my village preaching against Al Qaeda. I received numerous death threats from them. Then one day I was detained by the Americans."

He was adamant about his being against Al Qaeda, and it didn't seem like this was going to be a good button to push. So I explained to him, "At present, it looks bad for you. If you were truly not involved with Al Qaeda, you need to provide us with information about them. You should have no problem talking about them if you weren't a part of their organization."

Imam Ali just sat back, smiled, and asked, "What would you like to know about Al Qaeda?"

At first, I thought he might be trying to bait me into a theological argument, but then he went on, "I have nothing to hide, and I want to clean my village out of Al Qaeda. And if I can use you to do that, then let's talk."

This was music to my ears, exactly what an interrogator wants to hear. Finally, I had someone who was motivated to get rid of AQI operating in his village and had the knowledge to do so.

My newfound imam informant continued, "Prior to Operation Arrowhead Ripper, several AQI groups had moved into my area and set up their bases of operations. I will tell you the location of everyone I know, as well as what they have been doing."

When I heard Ali's reply, I knew it was going to take a while to get all the information he had. So I told him, "I will schedule us for a much longer session tomorrow. I'll also bring lunch and some maps of your area."

He replied, "I look forward to it."

With that, I ended the meeting and prepped myself for the following day's interrogation with our imam. My analyst and I were able to locate several color images of his village and the surrounding areas. These overlays were awesome— they were extremely clear and current and would help us identify the location of any AQI members that Ali might tell us about the following day.

As promised, for the next interrogation I brought in a roasted chicken with some fresh fruit and hot tea. I could see the delight in his eyes at the prospect of high-quality food. We had a leisurely lunch together, just basically shooting the breeze and enjoying ourselves as I worked my interrogator magic and continue to move Ali's allegiances toward us. I turned the conversation to a more serious note by asking my new imam friend, "What was going on in your village?"

He responded, "AQI moved into my area to create a new stronghold north of Baqubah to use as a safe house area for new fighters transitioning to the region."

Then I showed Imam Ali the color maps I had obtained the day before. "Could you show me the place you are talking about?"

He immediately pointed to a location near the outskirts of the village that was being used as an AQI medical clinic and stopover point. He told us, "The building is near a soccer field, but tucked away in the palm groves off the main road. This building usually gets passed by when the Americans come by on patrols." Using the color overlays of the area, it was simple to identify and easy to see how it had evaded previous attention. It was well off the road, and without an aerial photo, it would have been hard to find unless you knew to conduct a wide foot patrol through there.

Imam Ali then moved on to the next area. He showed us a compound near the main road that had two buildings on it. "One building is a home, and the second building is a garage. The home belongs to a man who works as a mechanic in the village. There are usually half a dozen cars parked inside his compound at any given time."

He pointed at the spot again with force and went on, "The garage is the location where AQI has been building VBIEDs that are getting used down in Baqubah."

This was significant information. FOB Warhorse, which was the main FOB near the Baqubah airport, had been getting hit hard with VBIEDs, as well as a number of the convoys operating inside of Baqubah and Al Khalis. Imam Ali continued, "AQI has been using this garage to build VBIEDs for some time, and members are surprised that the Americans do not already know about it."

I asked him, "Does AQI have any other buildings in ███████ village?"

He told me, "There is another home near the only school that is being used as a prison for AQI captives."

I saw this as the most pressing piece of information, so I pushed him for more details.

He explained, "There are several Sunni and Shi'a males and females who had been kidnapped and are being held at this location. AQI uses this house because it is on the outside of the village and close to the palm groves—in case they needed to make a hasty retreat."

This made me curious, and I asked, "Just how many people are working with AQI in this village?"

Ali replied, "The number is around fifty people or so."

I was rather surprised to learn there were so many. Although we are taught to hide our reactions, I am pretty sure that my eyebrows rose in concern before I could rein them in.

Imam Ali gave a very logical reason for the infiltration. "The village is very anti-American since the community has many former Ba'ath Party members who lost their prestige and positions when Saddam fell."

We continued talking for quite some time about the village. In addition to the number of people who worked for AQI in the village and the fact that the village had a VBIED factory and prison located in it, there was one more important piece of information I needed to know. "Are there any weapons supplies in your village? If so, where are they, and how many of them are there?"

Imam Ali let me know, "There are a number of weapon caches located around the village in the palm groves." He gladly showed me these locations as well.

He was very cooperative, telling me everything I asked him about his village with ease. It really seemed that he was passionate about removing Al Qaeda from his area because he made sure to tell me, "The two neighboring villages also have just as many AQI operating in them, and just as many weapon caches." This started a whole new set of conversations.

In all, Imam Ali identified the location of eight weapon caches, two AQI prisons, three safe houses, a VBIED factory, an IED assembly facility, over forty AQI members across three different villages…and a partridge in a pear tree.

My analyst and I spent about seven days and thirty hours of interrogations with Imam Ali obtaining this information. We generated eighteen intelligence information reports covering these three villages. When we finished, we just had to wait and see if any of the information would be acted upon.

Shortly before taking this case, I had gone to the Combat Stress Clinic on Camp Cropper, which was a clinic run by psychologists, counselors and a psychiatric doctor. Despite the Ambien I had started taking toward the beginning of my deployment to help me sleep, I was still having issues with achieving a restful slumber. In addition, my dreams were causing me more and more problems. I would go to sleep, but my mind just wouldn't turn off; I would run through the day's events, replaying interrogations and rehashing things I should or should not have asked, conversations with my fellow interrogators, and grotesque images people should never have to see.

After seeing one of the counselors for a couple of sessions, he referred me to see the psychiatrist for something that could help take the edge off. Shortly after this appointment, the doctor gave me Lexapro to help reduce my anxiety and hopefully allow me to sleep better and not feel so jumpy all the time. I had never taken a drug like this, but it was amazing. I went from never being able to turn my mind off and always feeling like I had a short fuse to suddenly just not caring…at all, about anything. Someone could tell me my dog died and I just wouldn't care. A rocket could land nearby and I would shrug it off like I'd never heard it. During interrogations, it made me feel completely emotionless. I was cold, direct and efficient. It was like the emotional aspect of the interrogation for me was turned off and suddenly I could completely focus on the tasks at hand.

****

At this point, I had been in Iraq for almost eight months and was coming up on my fifteen-day midtour break. Including training, I had been gone from my wife for fourteen months and we had only spent fourteen days together in that timeframe—not a whole lot of time to spend with your soulmate. Although I had been doing extremely well as an interrogator and had obtained some incredible intelligence, it was beginning to take its toll on me physically, emotionally, and psychologically.

I was burnt out and in desperate need of a break. My analyst and I had just collected some of the best intelligence we had received in a while from our imam, and now we were getting ready to head out on vacation. As I packed my bag and got ready to fly home for my midtour, I realized how immensely exhausted I was. My body was physically beaten, but so was my mind. My emotions were fried, and I had become so disconnected from reality outside of Iraq and interrogating terrorists. The only existence I had known for the last eight months was tracking down and killing or capturing these evil beings who at times bordered on no longer seeming human. Our intelligence reports were directly responsible for the death or capture of hundreds of Iraqis and countless detainees. Unfortunately, over two dozen Americans had been killed as well. Over time, the weight of all this responsibility was beginning to crush me like the weight of the world on Atlas's back. Now suddenly, I was being put on a plane and flown back to the real world.

My analyst was heading out the same time that I was. He was on his way back to Oklahoma, and I was on my way back to Florida. I remember walking off the military plane in Atlanta and just wandering through the airport heading to my next flight. I saw all these people talking and just enjoying life and feeling safe. It quickly dawned on me that I was truly secure as well, that for the first time in eight months, I wasn't carrying a pistol and rifle with me or ensuring that I knew where the closest bomb shelter was.

I was back in America and safe once again. Yet, as I boarded my next plane that would take me home, it just didn't feel real. Deep down in my stomach, I knew I had to go back to the sandbox, that this was just temporary. I also wanted to finish my mission. Part of me enjoyed being an interrogator, and I was making real progress in my area of Iraq.

Thankfully, once my plane had landed and my wife was waiting for me at the terminal, I forgot all about the desert and just focused on spending some much-needed quality time with her. I enjoyed my time at home, despite the fact that it was too short. My wife and I had a good experience visiting family in Chicago and just being home together. We went to Shula's Steakhouse and had perhaps the best steak of our lives. It was a peaceful reset of my mind—although the entire time, I absolutely dreaded returning to Iraq. The one positive thing I kept thinking was that after I returned to Iraq, I would only have a few more months left before this entire nightmare would be over and I could return to being a normal person. Though I enjoyed being an interrogator and I was extremely good at it, I was afraid of what it was doing to me emotionally and mentally. It was as if I was being transformed into this cold, heartless monster that only cared about accomplishing his mission at all cost.

Though I never crossed the line or broke any regulations in my interrogations, I felt as if I was getting closer to crossing that edge and slipping into that dark abyss. I wanted this experience to end, but like a strung-out druggie, I was addicted to the adrenaline rush of doing the job, and in some way, I resisted the end of the journey, wishing that the rush would also never expire. It's hard to explain to someone who has never done this type of job before, but the surge you get from having absolute and complete power over an individual is awe-inspiring. We collected information that led to thousands of raids and operations all across Iraq. We were wiping out the terrorist and insurgency through our individual actions. So, in the end, a lot of my time at home was spent struggling over these conflicting thoughts.

The Lexapro my doctor gave me did allow me to mellow out a lot during my midtour. With no major responsibilities, I just let go for a while. My wife told me that she thought I seemed a little spacy, but at least I was relaxing and we were enjoying our time together.

The next fifteen days went by like a dizzying blur, and before I knew it, I was back at the airport, making my long journey to Iraq. I arrived in Kuwait and was booked for the next flight to Baghdad. It was time to go back to the grind.
****

I remember sitting in the C-130 in Kuwait. It was August, and it had to be close to 130 degrees outside as our plane picked up speed down the runway. All of a sudden, there was a loud explosion and smoke. The plane stuttered and angled off the runway toward the sand. It quickly occurred to me that our flight was in trouble…I might not make it to Baghdad after all.

Smoke quickly filled up the cargo bay. The aircraft came to a screeching halt and the aircrew yelled at us, "Bail out of the plane! Use the front emergency door!"

We all frantically pushed and shoved our way out of the smoldering plane. As soon as we were out, we sprinted for the hills and then gathered to watch the smoke from a safer distance. As I looked at the frazzled group around me, an old saying came to mind: "There is no atheist in a foxhole." You could tell that there were some promises being made to live a better life as people were frantically fleeing from our C-130.

I found out later that while gaining speed on our take off, the rear tires had exploded and then caught on fire. Luckily, the plane slid off into the sand next to the runway and no one was hurt, but it sure scared the living daylights out of everyone on the plane.

After about half a day, our plane was repaired and we were once again on our way back to Baghdad. As if our initial takeoff wasn't enough, our plane received enemy fire as it flew into Baghdad. Someone in the Hay al Jihad neighborhood, which is near the Baghdad airport, shot a large-caliber machine gun at us as we began our final approach, forcing our plane to take immediate evasive maneuvers that would rival any rollercoaster ever built. The tracer fire streaked past us, and we then made an emergency landing as we attempted to avoid any further threats. I had had more than enough excitement for the day. I just wanted to get off the plane before I died.

Following our landing at Sather Air Base, a couple of guys from my squad met me at the airport to pick me up and take me out to dinner. Sather Air Force Base was by far the best DFAC around. Of course, it was also the only DFAC run by the Air Force, so it had better be good. We would routinely make our lunch or midnight meal runs to Sather. As we sat there eating our meal, I was telling my squad mates about my adventurous reentry to the country. I was in the middle of my story about the tire blowing up on our plane and swerving into the sand when out of nowhere, the incoming alarms went off. Suddenly, 1,500 people were no longer eating dinner but were instead huddled under the tables waiting for the impact. Three thundering booms could be heard, and the DFAC shook a bit with the vibrations, but there were no direct hits on us, so everyone got back up and resumed eating like nothing had happened. What a welcome party I was having that day. It was strange to think that to most of us who served in Iraq, this was a fairly normal experience, yet the average American would completely freak out. I guess you just got used to it over time.
****

I came back to a desk full of paperwork to weed through. In between dealing with some of the normal bureaucratic red tape, I had to spend the next couple of days figuring out what had transpired while I was gone. During the eighteen days that my analyst and I had been on midtour, a lot had happened. The reports we had generated from Imam Ali had resulted in an entire operation being planned

103

and carried out, called Operation Pericles, and it turned out to be a resounding success. The Army killed twenty-four AQI members, captured another twenty-three, and found six weapon caches. The weapon caches had over forty Katyusha rockets, twenty pounds of explosives, eighty 81mm mortars, six mortar tubes, two suicide vests, and two VBIEDs.

The capturing unit said it was one of the most successful operations in the Diyala River Valley and attributed the success directly to the intelligence my analyst and I had obtained. We even received a glowing letter of commendation from the capturing unit.

Of course, my management downplayed our success and told everyone, "They were just doing their job." No one was saying we weren't completing our assignments, but it would have been nice if our management had recognized some of us when we did an exceptional job that gained real, tangible results. I suppose our real satisfaction came in the form of knowing that we had captured or killed forty-seven AQI members.

However, the cases kept on coming, and there was no time to dwell on those thoughts. I received another interesting case of two detainees who had been captured for suspicion of being part of Jaysh al Mahdi. Both of them had been part of the new Iraqi Army as well; one of them held the rank of sergeant major, and the other was a corporal.

As I began to interrogate them, it became clear that the corporal was the one involved with Jaysh al Mahdi, and the sergeant major had just been at the wrong place at the wrong time. The sergeant major, Tariq, was by far and above the more cooperative one, so I spent most of my time with him.

As we discussed the situation in his area, he willingly divulged an immense amount of information about the internal problems with the Iraqi Army in the lower part of the Diyala province, which he called the northern Baghdad belt.

During the conversation, Tariq explained, "My army outpost was overrun by Al Qaeda about two months prior to my capture. We only had a total of eighty Iraqi Army soldiers commanded by a captain and me. Al Qaeda surrounded the outpost and bombarded us with mortars and rocket-propelled grenades for several days."

He took a deep breath, almost shuddered, and continued, "My army unit tried to fight them off for several days, but after taking numerous casualties and receiving no additional help from our headquarters, our captain ordered us to abandon our outpost and run."

In the process of abandoning the outpost, this Iraqi Army unit had left behind over sixty AK-47 assault rifles, a dozen PKC light machine guns and, even more disturbing, all the personnel files of the men who had been assigned to that outpost. They also left behind all their maps with all the exact coordinates of the smaller Iraqi Army outposts in the lower Diyala province. It was a complete operational security nightmare. Al Qaeda had just gotten an enormous amount of light and medium weapons and the coordinates for all of the local outposts, which would obviously greatly aid them in conducting future mortar and rocket attacks.

My analyst, Jeremy, and I were absolutely aghast at what had transpired. We immediately wrote up our intelligence reports and played a "wait and see" game of what would happen next. A week later, around 200 US Army troops moved through this particular area and did in fact find the burned-out outpost. They also came under heavy enemy fire and were forced to call in several air strikes and reinforcements to retake the village from the Al Qaeda fighters who had conquered it.

What astounded me the most was the fact that this Iraqi Army outpost had been completely overrun for several months, yet this was the first time we had learned of it. For me, this was another case in point of the incompetence of the Iraqi Army and the disunity that plagued its communications and leadership structure. Over time, it was becoming increasingly frustrating reporting these kinds of problems and not hearing any feedback as to whether the information was being used to help solve the issue. I, however, was just an interrogator with little ability to effect change...although I could try to help guide some of that change through the information I collected and the reports I published.

Chapter 14
A Rare Day Off

Before my midtour break, there had been precious few days off, despite the long hours. For whatever reason, things loosened up a little bit toward the end of the deployment. Word came down that we were going to have full days off, and my heart skipped a beat. I heard through the grapevine that there was a way for us to go to the chaplain service and sign up for a tour of the "Victory Over America" Palace and the Ba'ath Party Headquarters, so I jumped at the chance to go do some sightseeing.

My day off arrived, and a group of about twelve of us boarded a miniature bus to take the grand tour. All the sites we would be seeing were actually housed on the premises of the Victory Base complex, so it was comforting to think that we didn't have to exit the Green Zone in order to see something spectacular. The complex wasn't that large geographically, but at that point there were 200,000 people living there between the contractors and soldiers. The sea of humanity we were driving past was rather impressive. As we pulled up to an enormous grand building, it struck me that this had been so close to me the whole time, just out of reach.

The Victory over America Palace was enormous and opulent. The Grand Foyer as we walked in must have been at least three or four stories tall, lined with marble columns. Most of the walls were made of marble and covered in decorative letters and artwork. Saddam Hussein had begun the construction of this building after Desert Storm and claimed that it was in celebration of defeating the Americans. There were propaganda paintings, murals and mosaics everywhere that depicted scenes of Iraqis killing or bombing American forces.

We weren't able to tour the entire building. During the beginning days of Operation Iraqi Freedom, the palace had been hit with a bunker-busting bomb when we thought that we had good intel showing that Saddam Hussein would be there. Now there were large portions of the palace that were no longer structurally sound, and quite a bit of rubble was strewn throughout. There was no furniture in the building—it had likely been looted in between the time of the bombing and when Coalition Forces officially occupied Baghdad.

The irony of my visit was not lost on me. Here this palace had been built to put a thumb in the eyes of the Americans, and now, after we had occupied Iraq, I was able to walk freely through the building as a tourist. I took a bunch of photos to show my kids someday.

When we finished going through the building, we stood by a bunch of date trees, waiting for everyone else to catch up before our next stop, and one of the interpreters who had been on the tour with us decided that it would be fun to eat some dates straight from Saddam Hussein's date trees. He shimmied on up as if he were climbing a ladder, and soon we were all snacking on the royal dates.

The Ba'ath Party Headquarters were also impressive. The building was one story, but the ceilings were sixteen to eighteen feet tall. There was gold leaf along all the crown molding, and gold tiles in the mosaics on the walls. The building even had an indoor pool. Crystal chandeliers hung throughout the entire complex. It was so odd to think of the corrupt politicians who would surround themselves with these riches when so many of their people could barely survive.

This building had been one of the first to be hit during the Shock and Awe Campaign. In one of the conference rooms, there had been a meeting of 400 Ba'ath Party leaders. We had hoped that Saddam Hussein would be there. We couldn't walk into the room due to its compromised structural integrity, but from the doorway we could still see that the cruise missile we sent had been very effective in imploding the chambers. You could tell that the whole area had been consumed in a fireball. All that was left were remnants of burnt chairs.

The whole visit was rather empowering. For any flaws that we have as a nation, at least we don't have leaders that surround themselves in gold and jewels when their people are starving, and like Marie Antoinette tell their servants who do not have bread to eat, "Let them eat cake!"

Chapter 15
WMD

My fellow interrogators and I would sometimes sit down between our cases and swap stories about what was going on in the interrogation booth. It was a good way for us to glean insights into how to get the prisoners to open up, and sometimes it just made for fascinating drama that was hard to resist. One day while we were chewing the fat, Chang, who I considered to be one of the best interrogators, told us that his detainee had revealed a rather intriguing tidbit in exchange for a reduced sentence.

"You guys, my hadji just told me that he knows where a stash of WMD is."

"What?!" we shot back.

Since 2003, the media had been pumping nonstop stories explaining how there were "no weapons of mass destruction found in Iraq" and touting that the reason for going there in the first place had all been a sham.

Some of us were a bit more incredulous than others. One of the guys dismissed the story altogether, saying, "He's blowing smoke, Dude."

I wasn't sure it was real either, but Chang was smart, well educated, and decent at reading people. If he had managed to pull this information out and felt that it was legitimate, I figured there must be something to the story.

"He says that he used to work in Saddam's WMD program back in the nineties, and that there are still stockpiles left over. He told me that not all of the WMDs got turned over to the inspectors after the Gulf War in 1991."

"Write it up, for sure. And let us know what happens..."

Chang sent out the intel, and then we waited to see what would transpire next. A local unit actioned the report and did in fact discover a large cache of artillery shells filled with mustard gas. They took tons of pictures to document their find, so it wasn't long before we were sitting around looking at the photographs together. There they were, right in front of our eyes. They looked just like regular artillery rounds, but there was a gas symbol clearly painted on them as a warning. The shells looked old. I can't say for sure whether or not they were operational, but I can say with certainty that they existed. No one who saw those photos disputed that.

I suppose this wasn't a "smoking gun," in that these weren't new weapons. However, even if there hadn't been an active new WMD program, it did show that there was still a WMD capability there. Yet I never heard about this on the news. I would think that our President would want the American people to know that these discoveries were being made, but for years after this, there was silence.

In 2010, the movie *The Green Zone* came out, showing an action-packed drama that portrayed a journalist uncovering the giant "conspiracy" to keep America thinking that WMDs were the reason we went to war. The whole film is devoted to making its viewers think that going to Iraq was a mistake perpetuated on a lie. I have never been so angry while watching a movie before. I literally wanted to shout at the screen, "There *were* weapons of mass destruction there! How does no one know about this?"

In 2015, I read articles discussing the spread of ISIS in Iraq, explaining that ISIS was now using radiological materials and other forms of WMD that they captured while taking over territory in Iraq. You can't use something that didn't exist, right? I read another article that stated that the United States found more than 4,500 chemical munitions in Iraq after invading in 2003, although all of them appeared to have been manufactured before 1991. You can Google this—I am not making it up. There were weapons of mass destruction in Iraq, and it was covered up for more than a decade.

Chapter 16
Europe, Iraq, and the Horn of Africa

The very first case I was given when I arrived in Iraq was a man in his midthirties who had been detained at a traffic checkpoint. Hakim had been apprehended at the traffic checkpoint because his name was on a BOLO list, which stands for "be on the lookout," for suspicion of being a terrorist. When I first encountered him, I didn't realize that I had actually stumbled upon what might have been one of the most important men I would interrogate while in Iraq. He was so important, in fact, that I would still be dealing with him when I left for the States a year later.

Now, I may not be the most openly spiritual person, but the first time I met Hakim, I could sense the strong presence of evil. As he sat down across from me, I became uneasy. I would even say that I felt a little nauseous. His dark black eyes had an almost cobalt look to them that didn't seem quite human. When he looked me in the eyes for the first time, it was as if I were looking directly into the eyes of a demon, filled with rage and pure evil.

Looking over his file, I found that Hakim was a hardcore Al Qaeda operative who had been involved with them since the late '90s and also had some connections with Ansar al Islam. Continuing to glance through his paperwork, I read that Hakim had even attended the same mosque as several of the 9/11 hijackers prior to and after the attacks, which meant that he more than likely held to a strict Salafist ideology and probably knew several of the hijackers. My suspicion of him just continued to grow.

At first, I had no clue where to go with this detainee, so I started from the beginning. I asked him, "Hakim, what do you do for a living?"

He stared at me for a minute, trying to figure out what I was after and what he should or should not tell me. Then he grudgingly stated, "I owned a phone center in ▮▮▮▮ in Europe. I was here in Iraq visiting my wife and working out arrangements to take her to Europe with me."

As I talked a little bit further with him about his occupation in ▮▮▮▮, I discovered that Hakim and I had actually lived in the same city in Europe when I was part of a study abroad program. In fact, we might have even seen each other. He told me where he lived, and sure enough, it was within a few blocks of where I stayed. Once this common thread was discovered, he softened up a bit. Although my sense of this presence of evil around him never fully left, at least I had found some common ground and plenty of things to talk about. We chatted about a couple of the local restaurants and shops in the area and found that we had even frequented a number of them during the same time I was in school, adding further points we had in common.

I discovered after a little bit of research on Hakim that he had been involved in shipping vehicles from Europe to Iraq. Typically, vehicles shipped by those in terrorist organizations were either sold for profit and used to help fund AQI or in some cases were used as VBIEDs. AQI preferred to use expensive vehicles from Europe as VBIEDs because they were newer vehicles and attracted less attention from Coalition Forces. According to the information I found after some extensive digging, it appeared that my detainee might have been involved in this scheme.

I questioned Hakim on this topic, and he admitted, "Yes, I sent vehicles from Europe to Iraq on several occasions."

I immediately became excited because this was extremely important and, unbeknownst to Hakim, very incriminating. There had been previous reporting about Hakim's brother receiving vehicles from him and then selling the vehicles to help fund an AQI cell operating in the Diyala province. A couple of the vehicles had also been used as VBIEDs. During the forensics exploitation of one of the VBIEDs, they had recovered the VIN number from some of the parts of the vehicle. Those numbers had corresponded to a shipping manifest of vehicles Hakim had shipped to Iraq. Now I had Hakim confirming that he had sent vehicles to his brother—although he had no idea about the information I had on his brother, or how his information had in fact confirmed exactly what we thought was going on.

Despite having just made this connection in my head, I masked my enthusiasm so I could continue the conversation. I was curious as to how a person would ship vehicles from Europe to Iraq and asked Hakim, "How did you do it?"

Seeing that the question was nonincriminating, he proceeded to describe to me the process that he used to send the cars and trucks from Europe to Iraq. After we learned the procedures and the companies used in the vehicle shipments, we discovered that during a raid of Hakim's brother's home a year ago, there had been receipts from several shipping companies. Knowing the names of the companies from the receipts and the information Hakim had provided, we were once again able to validate his story and confirm the various companies used were the same companies Hakim had used.

I published a report with my findings, and within a couple of days, I received an evaluation citing the report as "high value" and was requested to obtain a variety of additional information from the detainee. This was my first time dealing directly with an outside agency that was interested in a case of mine. Throughout the intelligence community, there are a number of major intelligence consumers:

the Defense Intelligence Agency, the National Security Agency, the Central Intelligence Agency, the Federal Bureau of Investigation, and a myriad of other organizations within the military. Each was looking for something specific, and each of them sifted through intelligence reports until they found one that matched what they were looking for. In this case, the US Army European Command, or USAREUR, had become extremely interested in this report and in my case.

Because of the intertwining of Ansar al Islam and Al Qaeda, my case had now spread from Iraq into Europe. Though the two terrorist organizations had remained two separate entities up until around the end of 2003, it appeared that the two groups were now merging, or at least cooperating at a much higher level. In early 2002, a senior member of the Al Qaeda organization by the name of Abu Musab al-Zarqawi was invited into Iraq by the Ansar al Islam organization to begin spreading what was called at the time Jama'at al-Tawhid wal-Jihad in Iraq; this organization was later transformed into Al Qaeda in Iraq after the US invasion since it was being led directly by Zarqawi, who was a longtime Al Qaeda leader. Zarqawi had received his training in the late 1980s at an Al Qaeda training camp in Pakistan, which was run at the time by Osama bin Laden. During his training and subsequent fighting against the Soviets, he came into contact with other Al Qaeda members such as Ramzi Abbas and Khalid Shaikh Mohammed. Now Al Qaeda was cultivating their relationship with Ansar al Islam in an attempt to gain a foothold in another Middle Eastern country, and I had verifiable proof as several of my detainees corroborated pieces of the story.

To grow AQI, the organization needed money. Shipping vehicles from Europe to Iraq after the fall of Saddam was one of many ways Al Qaeda and Ansar al Islam financed the jihad against the Americans. Before I had arrived in Iraq, there had been several reports written about Hakim and his possible involvement in sending vehicles to Iraq to support AQI. Unknowingly, he had validated the previous reporting and indirectly confirmed his participation with Al Qaeda.

However, I continued to play along with this cover story and slowed the progression of the case down while my analyst and I continued to look for further information that might help us link our detainee to a greater web. We knew there were Al Qaeda cells in Europe, and we knew Al Qaeda had connections with the AQI groups here in Iraq. Now we just had to try to see if our detainee was linked to any of them and ascertain as much new information about it as we could.

I didn't have a lot of information to go on, which made for a slow-burning case. I had to coordinate everything I was doing with other intelligence elements in Europe. Most of the collaboration between me and USAREUR was done via email and a few long phone calls on our secured system. I would interrogate

Hakim and then contact USAREUR to let them know what I had learned. In some cases, I was collecting a vast amount of information that wasn't particularly helpful to us in Iraq, but it was extremely valuable to the group in Europe. They had very little in the way of intelligence about Hakim, his friends, or his activities for the last six years that he had been in Europe. My colleagues sent me multiple source-directed requests with questions specifically pertaining to what they were looking for. This allowed me to continue to question Hakim for the entire time I was in Iraq.

At one point, it seemed that Hakim's case was growing cold, but the network he belonged to was still of high interest to me, my analyst, and our newfound friends in Europe. My contacts in Europe informed us there were a couple of other prisoners of importance to them who were currently being held at Camp Bucca down in southern Iraq. They requested that the prisoners be pulled back to Camp Cropper and officially assigned to me and further interrogated. I felt honored that a major command outside of Iraq recognized my ability to obtain information and requested me by name to interrogate several prisoners that they had determined to be of high value.

Mohamed, one of the detainees who were being handed over to me, was also from Europe. He was an Iraqi Kurd who had had been living in the same city in Europe as me and Hakim.

It didn't take me long to get him to provide information of value to us about his activities back in Europe. He had been detained for two years at this point, so he felt no need to hide anything, believing that nothing he provided to me was going to be of value. However, even though the information he was giving away was several years old, the facts connected the dots on Hakim's case and the cases of several other detainees. As our conversation continued, I also began to link other people in Europe and in Iraq to this now-growing terrorist network still operating in Europe and Iraq.

My primary goal was to identify the people involved in the Ansar al Islam/Al Qaeda cell operating in Europe, as well as their connection with the various cells in Iraq. I was particularly interested in identifying how they were moving money from Europe to Iraq. I already knew from previous interrogations that Hakim had been involved in transferring vehicles from Europe to Iraq; now I was after something called a *hawala*, or financial house.

Hawalas are vicious little monsters for the CF intelligence community because they allow terrorists to transfer money without any means of tracking the transaction. The senders and the recipient have no direct contact. For example, if Abu Omar in Baghdad wanted to send $100,000 to his friend Mohammed in New

York, he would simply walk into his local hawala and let the owner, Abu Ishmael, know how much money he wanted to send and the destination. Then Abu Ishmael would look in his book of contacts, and once he found a man in New York he could work with, he would ask Abu Omar for $100,000 plus his usual fee. As soon as Abu Omar paid, he could go on his merry way. The owner would call his contact in New York and ask him to give $100,000 to Mohammed, which he would do right away. Abu Ishmael and his contact would settle up at a later time.

Unlike a Western Union, the money isn't wired or electronically transferred, which makes it much more difficult to track. The whole system is based on a complex series of interpersonal relationships and thus maintains its status of being "off the grid." It has been said that over a billion dollars a year is transferred throughout the Middle East via hawalas.

Hawalas really became a major factor when many Ansar al Islam cells formed all over Western Europe, acting as conduits to smuggle funds back to Iraq to support terrorist efforts. Yet Ansar al Islam was not a new organization or new to this type of smuggling activity. Ansar al Islam was the brainchild of Mullah Krekar, who converted an entire mountain village near the Iranian border, Biyara, to follow his new ideology, starting around the late 1990s. Because of his extreme charisma and convincing arguments, many Kurds who fled Iraq to escape the brutality of Saddam stayed loyal to the cause.

Even worse, Al Qaeda and Ansar al Islam had begun to unify their efforts in early 2000 through 2001. The two organizations were now working together to funnel money to Iraq and further terrorist activities prior to the US invasion, and dramatically increased their efforts after the invasion began. This complicated web had been used to send millions of dollars in support of the insurgency in Iraq, and we as Americans were more or less powerless to stop it since none of the money was being sent through standard banking processes. Worse yet, we had no idea how much currency or how many hawalas were involved.

However, I finally had a man sitting in front of me who was willing to explain everything he knew about the hawala system because he didn't think the information was worth anything. I tried to contain my glee as Mohamed responded, "I was a member of Ansar al Islam, and yes, I sent money from Europe to Iraq to help support my family."

Previous reporting had stated that Mohamed was sending money from Europe to support Ansar al Islam and Al Qaeda. When he admitted to sending the funds, it served to confirm suspicions that Mohamed might have been financing terrorist activities, because we had confirmed reports that his brother was a staunch member of Ansar al Islam who had been receiving the funds.

Prior to my interrogation of Mohamed, I had obtained a satellite image of the city in Europe that Mohamed had been living in, and I placed the map in front of him. With a casual conversational attitude, I asked, "Do you think you could show me where the hawala was that you used to transfer the money from ███████ to Iraq?"

Without hesitation or even a hint of nerves, he pointed to a building and said, "Yes, it was right here."

In my mind, I was jumping up and down. This was an absolutely amazing find. Our contacts in Europe had also confirmed that this hawala was being run and operated by Iraqi Kurds with ties to Ansar al Islam. We had identified the first major financial node being used to move money from Europe to Iraq.

While I was interrogating Mohamed, my analyst and I discovered that we had another prisoner, Musa, who had previously admitted to being a member of Ansar al Islam from the same area of Iraq that we had been targeting. I immediately placed this detainee on my hold list and started interrogating him in conjunction with Mohamed.

Musa had been a member of Ansar al Islam since it was founded. He had regularly attended religious classes taught by Mullah Krekar and Abu Abdullah al-Shafii, who was a student of Mullah Krekar and founder of the Ansar al Sunnah terrorist movement. He had a vast amount of information on the group.

Musa told me, "I worked at a medical clinic near ██████ village that provided medical support to wounded Ansar al Islam and Al Qaeda fighters. My medical clinic also provided medical and logistical support to two other Ansar and Al Qaeda training camps in and around the ██████ area."

I could tell that this man had the placement to give me some truly valuable information, so I asked Musa, "How did they obtain their financing?"

He replied, "We had supporters who lived in Europe, and they would send money to a hawala near Haladja. The money would then be picked up and spread around to the different groups."

I prodded, "Could you identify the location of the hawala if I were to show you a map of the city?"

He was hesitant at first, but after some further convincing and the promise of a phone call to his wife, Musa agreed to show us the location of the hawala he used.

Once I had learned the location, I went back and interrogated Mohamed on the subject again. As I stepped in the room, I could tell by the expression on his face that Mohamed was not particularly happy to see me. He was growing increasingly frustrated by my continual questions, and I think he suspected that I was piecing together large chunks of his criminal past. I asked him, "Incidentally, what city were you sending the money to in Kurdistan?"

He told me the name, and it was the same city as Musa had told me the previous day. I produced a map of the city and asked Mohamed to point out the location of the hawala.

At this point, he became somewhat obstinate and retorted, "I have not been to the city in numerous years."

I explained to Mohamed, "I know you have not been there in a long time, but all you need to do is point out the location of where you last remember it."

Reluctantly, he placed his finger on a spot on the map. As fate would have it, Mohamed identified the exact same location as Musa. It was incredible…we now had two different detainees from the same terrorist organization providing us the same information independently of each other. We also had a point of origin in Europe where the money was being collected and the exact location in Iraq where it was being received.

After thirty days and thirty-five interrogations, my analyst and I had finally obtained enough information from Mohamed and Musa to connect the dots between Europe and Iraq. We added this information to all the data we had collected from Hakim, and once again, we began some intensive collaboration with our European counterparts to see what direction to take next.

At this point, my analyst and I had been interrogating Hakim, Mohamed, and Musa for about nine months. We had conducted some seventy-five interrogations of them and nationally published twenty-one intelligence information reports regarding this European Al Qaeda/Ansar al Islam connection with Iraqi terrorists. It seemed like there was nothing else to gain from these three. However, just as we thought the case was going cold and we had found all we were going to find, we received a flash report from our European contacts that they had detained a friend of Hakim in ████████ for a traffic violation and then released him.

During his short detainment, they had discovered a wire transfer request made from Hakim's friend to a person named Ra'ad, in ████████ in the Horn of Africa. Our friends in Europe requested that I interrogate Hakim with this newest piece of information and try to determine if he knew who this Ra'ad was.

I knew it was going to be difficult to obtain the information that our European friends were looking for, so my analyst and I had to devise a new approach and plan. After we mulled this over for a day, an idea was born. We would choreograph a false flag approach. Hakim had continued to cling to his innocence and repeatedly insisted on speaking to someone from the German government. He had no legal status that required the German government to speak with him or obligated us to arrange such a meeting. However, I saw this as an opportunity to get him to give us the information we were looking for.

About seven months into our deployment, one of our former instructors from the advanced interrogation course back at Fort Huachuca had arrived at Camp Cropper and had begun working as a contract interrogator with us, his former students. Around the same time, another Army sergeant who had been in training with us back at Fort Huachuca also arrived. Both spoke fluent German; one was even a native speaker. My analyst and I talked with them and brought them into our little scheme. They quickly signed up. The plan was to have our former instructor play the role of a senior German official and be on the detainee's side, but explain to the detainee that he needed to cooperate so they could try and pull some strings to get him moved back to Germany. The younger sergeant was going to be the idealist crusader who saw it as her mission to find out who he was working with.

Our plan was to use a mix of the good cop/bad cop approach while throwing in the "we know all" approach to overwhelm him with the evidence against him. We wanted to convince Hakim that if he wanted to return to Germany, he would have to come clean. After we obtained permission to run the restricted approaches, the wheels were set into motion and we brought Hakim in for interrogation. Because this combination of approaches had never been run, and because our friends in Europe had stressed how important this information was, we had quite an audience watching.

I had Hakim brought into the interrogation room. He was clearly not happy to see me.

As he sat down, I told him, "I want you to know that I have gone to great lengths for you…I even went so far as to speak to the German government on your behalf." His eyes lit up. I had his attention now.

"In fact, I have two representatives of Germany here to speak with you today. In a minute, they're going to come in to the room here and I will introduce them to you. I expect you to be fully cooperative with them."

Hakim didn't speak, but his smile indicated his agreement.

Then I got up and walked over to the door, signaling to my coconspirators that it was time for them to enter. They walked into the interrogation booth dressed in civilian clothes, fully ready to play their parts.

I stepped out of the room and walked down the hall to the door that led to a small hallway between the interrogation rooms. Here I would be able to watch the interrogation through the one-way mirrors. There was already a crowd of people in the cramped hallway, eagerly watching as things got underway. As I observed my colleagues work their magic, I could see Hakim had gone from being elated to see them to being horrified by the accusations that were being made against him. The younger female sergeant was doing a superb job of playing bad cop— she was cursing him up one side and down the other, yelling at him and getting up in his face. It was quite a shock for an Arab man to have a woman treat him like that. It definitely threw him off.

My old instructor finally raised a hand and, in loud and commanding German, said, "Enough."

He then instructed her, "Leave the room for the minute and calm down."

Once she exited the room, he looked Hakim directly in the eyes and said, "I am sorry for the rude treatment my partner has just displayed. She is from the BND." Hakim would have known that the BND is the German equivalent of the CIA. He seemed to accept the explanation.

The instructor continued, "Hakim, I have been sent here to make a one-time deal with you. It is possible for you to be brought back to Germany with us and tried in a German court. If you are convicted, you will be held in our country, but if you are acquitted, then you would be allowed to stay in Germany."

This was exactly what Hakim had been telling me that he wanted for months—a chance to return to Germany and find safety away from the evil Americans. The ruse was working up to this point.

"In order for you to be transferred back to Germany, however, we need to make sure that we have answered all of our questions about you first. I will need you to be completely truthful with me."

Hakim nodded.

"I need to talk to you about your relationship with Ra'ad," my old instructor explained.

Hakim's eyes widened incredulously, and he started to deny ever meeting him.

"Look, I already know that you two know each other," he said, subtly tapping a thick folder on the table, "but I will need to know more if I am going to take you away from the Americans."

Hakim retorted, "OK, fine. I know Ra'ad. What do you really need to know?"

Back at my vantage point in the hallway, I was grinning ear-to-ear, knowing that our plan was working.

"When did you initially make contact with Ra'ad?" asked my old instructor.

Hakim replied, "I met him about six years ago, when I first arrived in Europe. He and I met at the local mosque that I prayed at. I was not good friends with him, but I do know who he is…"

My friend continued, "I need you to provide me with as much information as you can about Ra'ad."

Hakim grudgingly replied, "Ra'ad was more of a private man. I also did not agree with his religious views."

My friend pried, "What exactly do you mean by that?"

Hakim answered, "I thought Ra'ad followed more of a Salafist view of Islam. He was more extreme in his views."

"How often did you see Ra'ad at the mosque?" my friend asked.

"I only saw him when I went there to pray. We might talk, but only when we were at the mosque," Hakim explained, not realizing how valuable the information was that he was confirming for us.

Our friends in Europe had been monitoring this mosque and those that attended it for some time. During the observations, they had found that Hakim and Ra'ad met often at the mosque, though they knew very little of what they were discussing. What they did know was that the other members of this mosque were known Al Qaeda members.

The conversation continued for a little while. Once my friend had obtained the information we were after, he said, "Thank you, Hakim, for your cooperation. I will talk this over with the Americans and try to get you transferred back to Germany with us."

I went out in to the main hallway and conferred with my friends to go over what we had found and to ensure we hadn't missed anything and didn't need to follow up on anything else before our ruse was unmasked. Seeing that we had obtained everything we needed, I returned to the interrogation room with Hakim.

When he saw me, he immediately stiffened up like he had just won a great victory against me. He was elated that he had finally been able to talk with someone from the German government and was convinced he was going to be transferred to Germany. Knowing I had gotten everything I needed from Hakim, I simply said, "Thank you for your cooperation with my German colleagues. We will speak again at a later date."

Two days later, I called Hakim back in to be interrogated since I had to corroborate all the information from his last interrogation. As soon as he was seated, I broke the news to him. "You are not being transferred back to Germany. The Iraqi government wants to pursue charges against you."

He was immediately irate. I could see the anger burning in his eyes.

While giving Hakim the bad news, I noticed that he was taking an oddly strong interest in the pen I had sitting on the table. So, I asked, "What are you staring at?"

Hakim looked at me with his raging fire of hatred and hissed, "I'm staring at your pen."

Irritated, I barked out, "Why are you staring at my pen?"

Hakim was extremely annoyed at this point and yelled, "I was thinking of grabbing your pen and *stabbing* you with it!"

Seeing that I had my detainee at a breaking point, I pushed him further by picking up the pen and placing it directly in front of him. With a soft voice that grew to a yell, I said, "Feel free to try if you would like, but in the meantime, you will *answer my questions*!"

His agitation grew even more and beads of sweat appeared on his forehead—but I knew he wouldn't dare try something with all the guards around. While I had him good and upset, I grilled him over every detail of the previous interrogation. Utterly at a loss to resist anymore, he confirmed what I needed to know without too much incident.

After viewing the information my analyst and I had compiled on Hakim and his companions in Europe and reviewing the previous reporting on him, we came to the conclusion that Ra'ad was a newly identified member of the Al Qaeda organization that had been operating in Europe and was now in the Horn of Africa. We didn't think this was a stretch; we had enough information from Hakim to make that conclusion. We also had enough information to know that the mosque Hakim and Ra'ad attended was a major recruiting platform used by Al Qaeda. In addition, after a copy of the wire transfer was retrieved from his vehicle, there was strong suspicion that Hakim's other friend in Europe was a member of this Al Qaeda cell. I felt confident in identifying Ra'ad and Hakim's other European friend as part of Al Qaeda with some degree of certainty and sure that we had identified a previously unknown finance cell operating in Europe.

My analyst and I spent about six hours compiling all the information we had to date on this European connection and formulated a rather lengthy IIR about what we had found over our last nine months of interrogating these three detainees. We published our last report on this subject, concluding that we had obtained all useful information from these sources, and that there was an Al Qaeda/Ansar al Islam cell operating in Europe with connections in the Horn of Africa and Iraq. My analyst and I had been able to identify a web of terrorism that spanned three continents and over a dozen countries. We uncovered several new members of the terrorist organizations and the means they were using to transfer money to support global terrorism.

Shortly after our report was published, our colleagues in Europe gave my analyst and me an A evaluation, citing our intelligence information report as being of "major significance" in the global war on terrorism. During my year in Iraq, there were only four A evaluations given out by any government agency, so it was a big deal to be one of four. We both received a letter of commendation from US Army European Command for our efforts. I was also given an impact award by the Task Force 134 commander for superior intelligence performance. My analyst and I had conducted some four hundred hours of interrogations of these three detainees over a nine-month period, while still maintaining over a dozen other cases at a given time.

It was just unfortunate that there weren't enough interrogators to handle the immense number of detainees coming in. We might've been able to spend more time on this case and yielded even greater results if we'd had more resources, but you make do with what you have, not what you want.

Chapter 17
Returning Home and to Normality

After being gone from my wife for nearly 556 days, my time in Iraq was finally winding down. Our replacements had arrived, and we began the process of handing over our cases and ensuring the new guys knew what they were doing. Ironically enough, the interrogator that was replacing me had gone through the basic course with me at Fort Huachuca in Arizona. I was excited to see a familiar face, and even more excited that my friend Mike was going to be my replacement.

Mike was a great guy—he was in his early thirties and very well educated. He spoke Arabic well enough to get by and had a decent amount of life experience behind him. Those qualities made good key ingredients for him to become a successful interrogator.

I remembered my first day with the interrogator I replaced, and I determined that I was going to do a better job showing Mike the ropes. He needed to learn how to separate the wheat from the chaff. It was fun showing him some of the easy cases of people who would just cough up information if you asked, but he was also interested in the more difficult cases that would require a lot more effort. I made it a point to give Mike the best, most well-rounded experience I could while I was still there to help and mentor him. I thanked God that he was eager to learn, and more importantly, moldable. I felt like I could hand off my cases with confidence.

****

Not long after our replacements arrived, we made our preparations to leave Baghdad and start our long journey home. Unfortunately for me, I was among a small group of interrogators that was chosen to stay in Baghdad an additional twenty-four hours while the rest of our group flew down to Kuwait. It didn't bother me to spend an additional day in Baghdad, except for the fact that it was the last day of Ramadan, which is called "the night of power." This is when Allah is supposed to come down and smite the infidels from the earth.

Although Allah did not come down from heaven and strike us with lightning, the local Al Qaeda groups did launch a massive rocket and mortar attack on Camp Sather/BIAP Air Base and Camp Stryker, where I was living. Several of the bombs hit the airstrip, so maybe it was a good thing that I wasn't trying to travel that night. It was rather ironic in that here I was hours away from leaving Iraq, and we were getting the snot bombed out of us.

Throughout the next fifteen or so minutes, I just lay there in my bed listening to the thumping sounds of mortars and rockets hitting off in the distance, with the occasional mortar landing much closer. The walls of my room would shake a bit more from each successive boom. It sounds strange, but after living in an environment like that for so long, you just become numb to the fact that things are exploding nearby. I just rolled over and went back to sleep.

I remember sitting at the airport the following morning thinking to myself, "Wow, I made it." After everything that had happened, pure survival seemed like an accomplishment. Soon enough, our C-130 arrived and the few of us who had been left behind made our way out to the aircraft and boarded our freedom bird out of Iraq.

When we arrived in Kuwait, we met up with the rest of our group and were handed our plane itineraries that would take us home. At this point, I really began to get excited. Now I had a schedule of when I would arrive in the States. In only forty-eight more hours, I'd be on US soil, back home with my family and friends. My stay in Kuwait was short. It was just enough time for me to sit back and enjoy swapping stories with some of my friends about our cases before we all left for Baltimore. We salivated over discussions of what we were going to eat once we made it back to the US—everyone had steak dinners, pizza and alcohol on their minds. Some of the guys in our group had planned on taking a cruise or some other exotic vacation. My wife and I were looking at taking a cruise ourselves but planned on waiting until our anniversary in March.

As we all sat around chatting together, I realized that I had made some good friends while in Iraq. I was truly going to miss seeing and working with a number of these guys. We had all gone through so much the last eighteen months, and we had grown quite close to each other. I figured I would probably miss my roommate, Red, the most. He had become my best friend during the deployment, and I hoped that I would be able to see him again in the future.

After we had gone through customs, we boarded our final plane that would take us home. It was such a relief knowing that we were now officially on our way and this deployment was done. It had been the toughest thing I had ever endured, and it was now coming to a close.
****

Following nearly eighteen hours of traveling and layovers, we arrived in Baltimore at around 2100 hours and searched for a place to stay for the evening. I chose a hotel that was somewhat close to the airport and settled into my room. The first thing I did was order an American pizza, and then I called my wife. It was great to talk to her and not have an eight-hour time zone difference to deal with. It was also nice to be in a room of my own—one that was larger than the metal box I had lived in with two other guys for the majority of the last year—and to sleep in a bed larger than a twin size.

The following day, I boarded the plane that would take me back to Florida and home. However, even though my tour in Iraq was over, it didn't feel like it had really ended. While in Iraq, I had been suffering from extreme exhaustion and an inability to truly rest—this continued even after hitting stateside. I had no problem falling asleep, but I couldn't get any restful sleep. The Lexapro helped a lot, but when I returned to MacDill, our doctors couldn't prescribe that particular medicine and had to switch me to another drug that frankly had no effect on me. I could not get my brain to stop interrogating, even in my sleep. Though my body was home, my mind was not.

While in Iraq, I had worked an immense number of hours, either conducting interrogations, writing intelligence reports or researching. I essentially had no personal life or hobbies and was completely engulfed in my work. It was a strange experience when my wife and I went for a walk in the local mall near our house. Just six days prior to that, I had been interrogating an Al Qaeda cell leader about the location of several weapons caches, and four days ago our base was being rocketed during the last day of Ramadan. Now I was looking at new clothes and seeing the latest electronics that had come out while I was gone. It seemed too surreal for me. I had gone from working eighty hours a week to not working at all. It shouldn't come as a surprise that the adjustment to normality was rather difficult at times.

After I had my required two weeks of rest at home with my family, I was once again back to the old Air Force job that I had had prior to going to Iraq as an interrogator. Most of the people I had known previously were now gone; they had either deployed to Iraq themselves, or they had changed duty stations. Not only was I home and feeling like I had no purpose, I now had no friends either. I had just gone from a high-impact adrenaline-pumping job of interrogating terrorists to a dull, mundane job in which I felt I had little to no impact. It was a struggle to say the least.

I now had to try to develop new friends and relearn how to do most of my previous job. My supervisor was good about it for the most part. He tried to reintegrate me into the squadron and reintroduce me to a commander I had never met and a chief master sergeant that didn't even know I was a part of his squadron. I was the odd man out, and once people around me found out what I did in Iraq, the only thing they would ask me was, "So, did you torture anyone? How many people did you waterboard?" I really didn't know what to say or how to respond to a question like that. I never did any of those things, yet that appeared to be the perception that most of my fellow airmen had of me—that I was some maniacal torturer or something.

No one bothered to say, "welcome home" or "we're glad to have you back." What infuriated me the most was the fact that no one from my own squadron leadership or flight even showed at the airport to pick me up or welcome me home from the 556 days of grueling insanity. I truly felt like that soldier in that commercial on TV, walking through an empty airport and then walking through an empty city before someone walked up to him and shook his hand and said, "Welcome home." My first few weeks home and back at work were confusing, disappointing and frustrating.

Part of the reintegration back into the Air Force from the Army and Iraq was going back through medical processing. They became a little bit alarmed when they learned that I had been put on antidepressants and could not sleep I don't think they understood that I was not depressed, I was simply exhausted and edgy. A person can only have so many rockets and mortars go off near them before they develop a little restlessness, especially around loud noises or sudden movements. To add to that, my analyst and I were responsible for the deaths of hundreds of Iraqis, and close to thirty Americans had been killed during intelligence-driven missions from our interrogations. I know we were doing our jobs, and I am confident we saved American and Iraqi civilians lives, but when you stop and think about it, that's a lot to carry on your shoulders. When you couple that with the numerous images of beheadings, dismembered and mutilated bodies and the stories I had to hear while interrogating hundreds of terrorists, it's not too hard to understand why I might have been feeling a little off sometimes.

After the medical group had their fun with me, it was time for the required evaluation at the mental health clinic. What a name—mental health clinic. Honestly, I thought it would be interesting having to go see a civilian psychiatrist...two trained manipulators sizing each other up and trying to figure each other out. The doctor assigned to me was rather quizzical too, and I found it amusing to watch as she prodded and probed me just as I had done to the terrorists I had previously interrogated. I wasn't really sure what to say, though. There were so many things I just couldn't talk about with her because the information was classified, and there were numerous other things that I frankly didn't think she needed to know about. Part of being an interrogator was playing my cards close to my chest and providing as little information as possible while obtaining as much information as I could.

It was difficult to turn off my interrogator training and not evade her questions. In fact, I had to resist the strong urge to ask her probing questions of my own. During my first appointment, rather than spending my time talking to her and answering her openly, I found myself slipping into my interrogator role. Through a series of questions, I had her telling me all about what was wrong with the medical command she was working with and what she thought could be done to make it better. I suppose I should have felt bad about outmaneuvering her like that, but it was so easy for me to do and second nature to turn that attention away from me and back toward something else. However, the second time we met, she realized what I had done and made it clear we were there to talk about me and not her.

I found it interesting that after several appointments with this shrink, she said I had mild depression and moderate to severe post-traumatic stress disorder. I wondered, *How does she know if I have PTSD or not? What does it mean if I do have it, and what am I supposed to do about it?*

However, no one legitimately explained to me what this meant or what actions I needed to take going forward. So, I just kind of blew it off and continued on with my job. As if I didn't have enough of a stigma from being an interrogator, I now had this mental health label added to my military file as well. Rather than being able to wear this job as an interrogator and my accomplishments in Iraq as a badge of honor, it felt more like a black mark and something that the military was embarrassed to recognize that we did.

My friend Red didn't have it so easy either. He couldn't report that he'd not slept well since the end of training. The military machine has a built-in bias against those with problems, especially if they are on the Personnel Reliability Program. He can't even take aspirin without approval. Reporting this would drop him from Personnel Reliability Program status, or perhaps get him med-boarded out. He keeps the secret to this day until he retires. Fortunately, by the time this book is released, that will be very soon.

We will never have a normal conversation again as we did before training. We tend to manipulate others now without thinking. We look at the world differently. Catching the general public at large in a lie is common place. We just know the signs now. It makes life hard to cope with. You'd be surprised how many times a day the man or woman next to you will tell a lie, even stupid lies. We just bite our tongues and move on.
****

I only had seven months left on my enlistment once I arrived back home from Iraq. I needed to make some decisions about reenlisting for another four years or separating from the military and taking my chances in the private sector. After praying about it and talking it over with my wife for several months, and facing a potential redeployment again in six months instead of the required twelve-month break, we came to the conclusion that it would be best for me to leave the military and pursue opportunities elsewhere. The last thing I wanted to do was fill in for some NCO who had a newfound medical problem that prevented him from doing his deployment and forced me to take his place.

In late May 2008, I separated from the Air Force and began my journey back into the civilian world. I felt good about leaving the military when I did because I had done my part. We were now winning the war in Iraq and had laid the groundwork for the US to leave that country. I felt we interrogators had played a pivotal role in America achieving that objective. We were, after all, the ones obtaining the intelligence that was allowing us to win. I had done over 2,200 hours of interrogations in Iraq and was among the highest producing HUMINT collectors during the war. It was now time for me to put my rifle down, fold my uniforms up for the last time and let someone else step into the breach. Though the global war on terror was not over, I felt comfort that my part in it was.
****

So once again, I'd become just an ordinary guy. You wouldn't know that I had been an interrogator by looking at me, but I played an important part once. I might seem like the guy you'd take your taxes to, but once upon a time, I saved American lives by having dinner with a terrorist. The rest of the world may think that interrogators have an ugly profession or view us as evil torturers or monsters, but I wish there were more guys out there like us, willing to answer the call and do what needs to be done for the sake of our country. Maybe the next time you have a cup of coffee in your favorite coffee shop, you will remember my story and be thankful that there is someone else out there having coffee with a terrorist from the "most wanted" list, keeping you safe.

Epilogue
Notes from the Wife of an Interrogator

I could see in my husband's eyes that something was different from the moment he returned home. He was not the same man I had sent off to the battlefield so many months ago. I had noticed it when he was home on his midtour as well. He was vacant, aloof and withdrawn. At that time, I chalked it all up to the utter exhaustion he must be experiencing from working more than twelve hours every day for multiple months in a row. The Air Force did not provide me with any sort of training regarding dealing with a completely new person in our home, but I had enough sense to realize that his readjustment would take some time.

However, days turned into weeks, and weeks turned into months. This man that I loved, that I cared for so deeply, was often short with me—lacking patience at completely odd times, and sometimes in public. He would forget things that we had talked about recently, and tasks that used to be his responsibility fell through the cracks. He found escape in an online video game community called EVE online; I think the missions within the game allowed him to feel a sense of purpose again, but he will admit now that his obsession with this game went well beyond a normal level of recreational hobby. I was too embarrassed to talk to any of my friends at church about the real problems that were lurking underneath the surface. It was only after I began nursing school and started to learn about PTSD that I really understood some of what was happening to James. A variety of things triggered memories of war—everything from smells to loud noises to specific phrases I might say—and flooded him with adrenaline, activating the "fight or flight" response.

The VA did provide him with meds, of course, but I just basically felt like he was drugged up and shipped off to live his life. There were sometimes problems getting the medications in the mail, and he didn't always tell me this was the case—just so you know, if you ever start a medication for psychological well-being, you should never, repeat *never*, stop it suddenly. The consequences are horrendous: sweating, heart pounding, mood swings, and extreme agitation. There were a few times that I almost threw in the towel on our marriage, and it mostly stemmed from times that the medication hadn't been there for him in time.

Despite my subsequent training as a nurse, I didn't always know how to deal with these issues. It's one thing to know that a patient has PTSD and respond accordingly, and entirely a different matter to live with someone who deals with it every day. Until the medications were worked out, there would often be screaming in the middle of the night, thrashing, fighting with "the enemy." During the day, I sometimes felt like *I* was the enemy. It was very difficult.

Why do I share this immensely personal window into our relationship? Because I have seen so many of my friends deal with this same problem, and it is not inevitable that life must remain an intense struggle. My husband was resistant at first to seeking any kind of counseling…many people are. They are afraid of the stigma surrounding mental health. They don't like to have their head shrinked. However, when he finally broke down and sought help, he gained some valuable techniques for dealing with triggers and readjusting to normal life after such a fast-paced action-packed year. There is a newer type of counseling out now called eye movement desensitization and reprocessing, or EMDR, that many are finding helpful.

Just this year, we found a ministry that combined prayer and more conventional therapy techniques into a free retreat for soldiers and their spouses. It was life changing. I could see in his face that he felt unburdened, lighter. We had split up at a certain point into different rooms. I was so curious what they talked about in their room, but I tried not to push him into talking about it before he was ready. While we were still at the retreat, he suddenly told me, "I want to finish the rewrite of the *Dinner with a Terrorist* book soon. That way, I can finally close the door on that chapter of my life."

Then one day, he was sharing with me some of the traumatic memories he had dealt with—some that were in this book, and some that were excluded—and he told me that he had been trying to pray and ask God to show him Jesus in each of those memories. "I think about myself in that situation, and I see Jesus there now—holding back that missile from exploding and hitting me, or sitting next to me in the interrogation booth—and now those memories don't seem so traumatic. All I see is Jesus."

Every day, many veterans commit suicide. There is debate about the exact number, but even one would be too many. The sad truth is that the VA is very lacking in its assistance to veterans who struggle with depression or PTSD. Many, like my husband, are drugged up and pushed out, never to receive any legitimate counseling. Spouses are not counseled *at all*, and many marriages break up when they are unable to deal with these changes. However, there are many good ministries and counselors out there who will assist veterans, and if you look, you can even find help that is free or covered by insurance. Please, I implore you, if you read this book and know that you have struggled, seek help, and don't stop until you find the help that will work for you. Seek help for your family too; spouses are not immune.

If you know someone who has returned from the battlefield, please, give them a call. Check on them, even if they say that everything is OK. Ask honest questions and be prepared for honest answers that may not be pretty descriptions of a hunky-dory existence. If we all were to reach out to even just one struggling veteran, maybe we could save a life.

From the Authors

Miranda and I sincerely hope you have enjoyed this book. We are always working on writing more; our current projects are a military thriller series, The Monroe Doctrine, and a military sci-fi series, The Rise of the Republic. To find more of our books, please visit Amazon.

If you would like to stay up to date on new releases and receive emails about any special pricing deals we may make available, please sign up for our email distribution list. Simply go to https://www.frontlinepublishinginc.com/ and sign up.

If you enjoy audiobooks, we have a great selection that has been created for your listening pleasure. Our entire Red Storm series and our Falling Empire series have been recorded, and several books in our Rise of the Republic series and our Monroe Doctrine series are now available. Please see below for a complete listing.

As independent authors, reviews are very important to us and make a huge difference to other prospective readers. If you enjoyed this book, we humbly ask you to write up a positive review on Amazon and Goodreads. We sincerely appreciate each person that takes the time to write one.

We have really valued connecting with our readers via social media, especially on our Facebook page https://www.facebook.com/RosoneandWatson/. Sometimes we ask for help from our readers as we write future books—we love to draw upon all your different areas of expertise. We also have a group of beta readers who get to look at the books before they are officially published and help us fine-tune last-minute adjustments. If you would like to be a part of this team, please go to our author website, and send us a message through the "Contact" tab.

You may also enjoy some of our other works. A full list can be found below:

Nonfiction:
Iraq Memoir 2006–2007 Troop Surge
Interview with a Terrorist (audiobook available)

Fiction:
The Monroe Doctrine Series
Volume One (audiobook available)
Volume Two (audiobook available)
Volume Three (audiobook available)
Volume Four (audiobook still in production)

Volume Five (available for preorder)

Rise of the Republic Series
Into the Stars (audiobook available)
Into the Battle (audiobook available)
Into the War (audiobook available)
Into the Chaos (audiobook available)
Into the Fire (audiobook still in production)
Into the Calm (available for preorder)

Apollo's Arrows Series (co-authored with T.C. Manning)
Cherubim's Call (available for preorder)

Crisis in the Desert Series (co-authored with Matt Jackson)
Project 19 (audiobook available)
Desert Shield
Desert Storm

Falling Empires Series
Rigged (audiobook available)
Peacekeepers (audiobook available)
Invasion (audiobook available)
Vengeance (audiobook available)
Retribution (audiobook available)

Red Storm Series
Battlefield Ukraine (audiobook available)
Battlefield Korea (audiobook available)
Battlefield Taiwan (audiobook available)
Battlefield Pacific (audiobook available)
Battlefield Russia (audiobook available)
Battlefield China (audiobook available)

Michael Stone Series
Traitors Within (audiobook available)

World War III Series

Prelude to World War III: The Rise of the Islamic Republic and the Rebirth of America (audiobook available)
Operation Red Dragon and the Unthinkable (audiobook available)
Operation Red Dawn and the Siege of Europe (audiobook available)
Cyber Warfare and the New World Order (audiobook available)

Children's Books:
My Daddy has PTSD
My Mommy has PTSD

Acronym Key

AQI	Al Qaeda in Iraq
BIAP	Baghdad International Airport
BOLO	Be on the Lookout
CF	Coalition Forces
CRAM	Counter Rocket, Artillery and Mortar
CW3	Chief Warrant Officer, Level 3
DFAC	Dining Facility
DIA	Defense Intelligence Agency
DoD	Department of Defense
FBI	Federal Bureau of Investigations
FOB	Forward Operating Base
HUMINT	Human Intelligence
HVI	High-Value Individual
IBA	Individual Body Armor
ICE	Interrogation Control Element (office where the interrogators and analysts work)
IED	Improvised Explosive Device
IIR	Intelligence Information Report
IRGC	Iranian Revolutionary Guard Council
ISIL	Islamic State in the Levant
JAM	Jaysh al Mahdi
JIDC	Joint Intelligence Defense Center
MMA	Mixed Martial Arts
NCO	Non-Commissioned Officer
PIR	Priority Information Reports
PODS	Portable on-Demand Storage
PT	Physical Therapy
PTSD	Post-Traumatic Stress Disorder
RPG	Rocket-Propelled Grenade
SHU	Separation Housing Unit
SSG	Staff Sergeant
SUV	Sports Utility Vehicle
TIF	Theater Internment Facility
USAREUR	US Army European Command
VA	Department of Veterans Affairs
VBC	Victory Base Complex

VBIED   Vehicle-Borne Improvised Explosive Device
VIN   Vehicle Identification Number

www.ingramcontent.com/pod-product-compliance
Lightning Source LLC
Chambersburg PA
CBHW071008120626
46546CB00003B/996

* 9 7 8 1 9 5 7 6 3 4 2 5 8 *